GoodFood

101 STORE
D0480900
S

Published in 2008 by BBC Books,
an imprint of Ebury Publishing
A Random House Group company

Copyright © Woodlands Books Ltd 2008
All photographs © BBC *Good Food*
magazine 2008
All recipes contained within this book first
appeared in BBC *Good Food* magazine

All rights reserved. No part of this publication
may be reproduced, stored in a retrieval system,
or transmitted in any form or by any means,
electronic, mechanical, photocopying, recording
or otherwise, without the prior permission of the
copyright owner.

The Random House Group Limited
Reg. No. 954009

Addresses for companies within the
Random House Group can be found at
www.randomhouse.co.uk

A CIP catalogue record for this book is available
from the British Library.

The Random House Group Limited supports
The Forest Stewardship Council (FSC), the
leading international forest certification organization.
All our titles that are printed on Greenpeace
approved FSC certified paper carry the FSC logo.
Our paper procurement policy can be found at
www.rbooks.co.uk/environment

To buy books by your favourite authors and
register for offers visit www.rbooks.co.uk

Printed and bound by Firmengruppe APPL,
aprinta druck, Wemding, Germany
Colour origination by Dot Gradations Ltd, UK

Commissioning Editor: Lorna Russell
Project Editor: Laura Higginson
Designer: Annette Peppis
Production: David Brimble
Picture Researcher: Gabby Harrington

ISBN: 9781846075674

GoodFood

101 STORECUPBOARD SUPPERS
TRIPLE-TESTED RECIPES

Editor
Barney Desmazery

BBC
BOOKS

Contents

Introduction

With our busy schedules and active families, it feels like we have less time than ever to prepare healthy home-cooked meals; readers often ask the *Good Food* team for quick mid-week meal ideas. So what's the solution? The good news is that a well-kept storecupboard can make life easier – with a few staples in the fridge, freezer and larder, a speedy meal is always moments away.

To help make cooking stress-free when you're short of time, we've picked 101 recipes from *Good Food* magazine that use everyday ingredients. The recipes can be created to feed one, two, or a hungry family or group of friends. Including complete storecupboard stand-bys, easy one-pot meals, quick snacks, midweek meals, special-occasion dishes and made-in-minute puddings, there's a clever, quick idea to suit every mealtime.

As well as providing new ideas for store-cupboard classics like pasta and eggs, the recipes in this book have also been chosen to inspire you to try something different. Each recipe has been created and tested by the *Good Food* team to ensure nutritionally balanced, eco-nomical and speedy dishes, so you can enjoy fast food that's good for you too.

Barney Desmazery
Good Food magazine

Notes and conversion tables

NOTES ON THE RECIPES

• Eggs are large in the UK and Australia and extra large in America unless stated otherwise.

• Wash fresh produce before preparation.

• Recipes contain nutritional analyses for 'sugar', which means the total sugar content including all natural sugars in the ingredients unless otherwise stated.

OVEN TEMPERATURES

Gas	°C	Fan °C	°F	Oven temp.
¼	110	90	225	Very cool
½	120	100	250	Very cool
1	140	120	275	Cool or slow
2	150	130	300	Cool or slow
3	160	140	325	Warm
4	180	160	350	Moderate
5	190	170	375	Moderately hot
6	200	180	400	Fairly hot
7	220	200	425	Hot
8	230	210	450	Very hot
9	240	220	475	Very hot

APPROXIMATE WEIGHT CONVERSIONS

• All the recipes in this book list both imperial and metric measurements. Conversions are approximate and have been rounded up or down. Follow one set of measurements only; do not mix the two.

• Cup measurements, which are used by cooks in Australia and America, have not been listed here as they vary from ingredient to ingredient. Kitchen scales should be used to measure dry/solid ingredients.

SPOON MEASURES

Spoon measurements are level unless otherwise specified.

- 1 teaspoon (tsp) = 5ml
- 1 tablespoon (tbsp) = 15ml
- 1 Australian tablespoon = 20ml (cooks in Australia should measure 3 teaspoons where 1 tablespoon is specified in a recipe)

APPROXIMATE LIQUID CONVERSIONS

metric	imperial	AUS	US
50ml	2fl oz	¼ cup	¼ cup
125ml	4fl oz	½ cup	½ cup
175ml	6fl oz	¾ cup	¾ cup
225ml	8fl oz	1 cup	1 cup
300ml	10fl oz/½ pint	½ pint	1¼ cups
450ml	16fl oz	2 cups	2 cups/1 pint
600ml	20fl oz/1 pint	1 pint	2½ cups
1 litre	35fl oz/1¾ pints	1¾ pints	1 quart

Balsamic glaze is a rich, sweet syrup made from reduced balsamic vinegar. You will find it in large supermarkets, usually next to the vinegars. This recipe can easily be doubled.

10-minute steak and blue cheese wrap

1 tbsp olive oil
1 x 140g/5oz sirloin steak
1 small red onion, thinly sliced
½ red pepper, seeded and sliced
squeeze balsamic glaze or drizzle of balsamic vinegar
1 small soft flour tortilla
25g/1oz Stilton or dolcelatte
handful of rocket or baby spinach leaves

Takes 10 minutes • Serves 1

1 Heat the oil in a hot frying pan, season the steak, then fry with the onion and pepper for 4 minutes over a moderate heat. Stir in the balsamic glaze/vinegar, continue to cook for 1 minute, then remove from the heat.
2 Warm the tortilla. Slice the steak into thin strips, then tip it back into the pan with any meat juices and mix with the veg. Spoon the mixture over the middle of the tortilla, crumble over the cheese, then scatter with rocket or spinach leaves. Fold to make a wrap, cut in half and serve straight away.

• Per serving 686 kcalories, protein 48g, carbohydrate 66g, fat 28g, saturated fat 10g, fibre 5g, sugar 12g, salt 1.43g

Bacon makes a brilliant alternative here to the more traditional
Chinese barbecue pork. Serve these as a starter or a nibble.

Barbecue pork buns

85g/3oz sugar
500g pack white bread mix

FOR THE FILLING
1 tbsp sunflower oil
12 rashers rindless streaky
unsmoked bacon, chopped
knob of fresh root ginger, peeled and
chopped
2 garlic cloves, chopped
2 tbsp soy sauce
3 tbsp clear honey
3 tbsp tomato purée
1 egg, beaten, to glaze

Takes 50 minutes, plus rising
Makes 12

1 Mix the sugar and bread mix in a bowl, add water according to the packet instructions. Bring the dough together and knead it on a floured surface until smooth. Put it into a large bowl, cover with cling film and leave in a warm place until doubled in size.

2 To make the filling, heat the oil in a pan and fry the bacon until crisp. Add the ginger and garlic and fry for 1 minute. Add the soy, honey and tomato purée.

3 Heat the oven to 220°C/fan 200°C/gas 7. Turn out the dough and knead, then pull into 12 balls. Flatten each one with your hands, then put a teaspoon-sized blob of the filling in the middle. Draw the dough up and pinch it closed like a purse, then turn the bun over and sit it on a large baking sheet. Cover with oiled cling film and leave to rise. Brush with egg and bake for 20 minutes.

• Per bun 512 kcalories, protein 19g, carbohydrate 82g, fat 14g, saturated fat 5g, fibre 3g, sugar 24g, salt 3.78g

This easy-to-make soup is high in fibre, a good source of vitamin C and counts as 2 of your 5-a-day.

Minestrone in minutes

100g/4oz spaghetti
1 litre/1¾ pints hot vegetable stock
400g can chopped tomatoes
350g/12oz frozen mixed vegetables
4 tbsp pesto, a drizzle of olive oil
and some coarsely grated
Parmesan, to serve

Takes 10 minutes • Serves 4

1 Take the spaghetti and wrap it in a clean tea towel and, holding it with both hands, bash it to break it into small pieces. Set aside.

2 In a medium-sized pan, bring the stock to the boil with the tomatoes, then add the spaghetti and cook for 6 minutes or until almost al dente.

3 A few minutes before the pasta is ready, add the vegetables and bring back to the boil. Simmer for 2 minutes or until everything is just cooked. Serve the soup ladled into bowls, drizzled with pesto and oil, and sprinkled with Parmesan.

• Per serving 162 kcalories, protein 8g, carbohydrate 30g, fat 2g, saturated fat none, fibre 6g, sugar 8g, salt 0.54g

These muffins are yummy warm, but they also keep well for a few days – which makes them ideal for lunchboxes.

Welsh rarebit muffins

225g/8oz self-raising flour
50g/2oz plain flour
1 tsp baking powder
½ level tsp bicarbonate of soda
¼ tsp salt
½ level tsp mustard powder
100g/4oz strong cheese, half grated, half cubed
6 tbsp vegetable oil
150g/5½oz Greek yogurt
125ml/4fl oz milk
1 egg
1 tbsp Worcestershire sauce

Takes 40 minutes • Makes 12

1 Preheat the oven to 200°C/fan 180°C/gas 6 and line a 12-hole muffin tin with 12 muffin cases. Mix together the self-raising and plain flours, baking powder, bicarbonate of soda, salt and mustard powder in a bowl.
2 In a separate bowl, mix the cheese, oil, yogurt, milk, egg and Worcestershire sauce.
3 Combine all the ingredients and divide the mixture among the muffin cases. Bake in the oven for 20–25 minutes or until golden. Remove and cool slightly on a wire rack.

• Per muffin 189 kcalories, protein 6g, carbohydrate 19g, fat 11g, saturated fat 4g, fibre 1g, sugar 1g, salt 0.79g

Flour tortillas keep well in the freezer and make a useful
alternative to bread.

Spicy bean and avocado tostados

4 flour tortillas
400g can refried beans
big pinch of cayenne pepper
200g can kidney beans in water,
drained and rinsed
2 handfuls of cherry tomatoes,
quartered
50g/2oz Cheddar, grated
1 green chilli, thinly sliced
1 avocado, halved, stoned and sliced
handful of coriander leaves, to serve

Takes 15 minutes • Serves 4

1 Heat the grill to Medium–High. Put
2 tortillas on to a large baking sheet and
grill for 2 minutes.
2 In a bowl, combine the refried beans,
cayenne pepper, kidney beans and cherry
tomatoes, then divide half the mix between
the tortillas. Scatter with half of the cheese
and half of the sliced chilli, then grill again
until the cheese melts.
3 Grill the remaining tortillas and repeat the
method using the rest of the ingredients.
4 Lift the tostados on to plates and serve
topped with the avocado and coriander.

• Per serving 355 kcalories, protein 16g, carbohydrate
43g, fat 14g, saturated fat 4g, fibre 4g, sugar 3g,
salt 2.35g

A batch of this simple, healthy dip can be kept in the fridge for up to 3 days.

Smoked mackerel dip

250g pack smoked mackerel fillets
142ml carton soured cream
1 bunch spring onions, trimmed and finely chopped
4 tsp horseradish sauce
selection of crunchy raw vegetables, to serve

Takes 10 minutes • Serves 2

1 Carefully peel away the skin from the mackerel fillets and finely flake the fish.
2 In a mixing bowl, stir the flaked smoked mackerel, soured cream and spring onions together to make a textured dip, then stir in the horseradish. Spoon into a serving bowl and serve with sticks of raw veg for dipping.

• Per serving 561 kcalories, protein 25g, carbohydrate 5g, fat 49g, saturated fat 17g, fibre 1g, sugar 5g, salt 2.23g

This is a delicious, healthy chilled soup that's perfect for hot summer days.

Quick gazpacho

1 red pepper
1 red chilli
250ml/8fl oz passata
1 garlic clove, crushed
1 tsp sherry vinegar
juice of ½ lime

Takes 10 minutes • Serves 1

1 Peel the skin off the red pepper with a vegetable peeler, seed it and chop it up. Cut the chilli in half, scrape away the seeds and chop the flesh.

2 In a blender (or with a stick blender), whiz together the passata, red pepper, chilli, garlic, sherry vinegar and lime juice until smooth. Season to taste and chill until cold. Serve in a soup bowl with a few ice cubes.

• Per serving 126 kcalories, protein 5g, carbohydrate 26g, fat 1g, saturated fat none, fibre 3g, sugar 18g, salt 1.26g

This clever salad is wonderful on it's own or as part of a buffet.

Lentil and red pepper salad

400g can lentils
5 roasted red peppers from a jar, chopped
handful of radishes, sliced
handful of olives
2 tbsp balsamic vinegar
4 tbsp olive oil
2 Little Gems
200g/7oz feta

Takes 15 minutes • Serves 2 generously

1 Empty the lentils into a sieve, wash well under cold running water and leave to drain.
2 Tip the lentils and peppers into a bowl along with the radishes, olives, vinegar and oil, and mix well so that all the ingredients are coated in the dressing. Season to taste.
3 Separate the lettuce leaves and scatter them over a large plate. Spoon over the lentil salad and evenly crumble the feta over everything.

• Per serving 634 kcalories, protein 22g, carbohydrate 29g, fat 49g, saturated fat 14g, fibre 9g, sugar 12g, salt 6.81g

These cheesey nachos are great for nibbling on. The salsa can also be used as a healthy dip, served with vegetable sticks.

Anytime sweetcorn and tomato nachos

1 avocado
200g can sweetcorn,
rinsed and drained
200g can chopped tomatoes
½ onion, finely chopped
large handful of coriander leaves,
chopped
1 bag lightly salted tortilla chips
big handful of grated Cheddar

Takes 15 minutes • Serves 4

1 Cut lengthwise across the avocado and around the stone, then twist and separate the two halves. Scoop out the stone. Use a sharp knife to make diagonal cuts along one half, then make cuts the other way so that you end up with a criss-cross effect. Run a large spoon around the skin, releasing the avocado chunks. Do the same with the other half.

2 Heat the grill to High. Mix the avocado with the sweetcorn, tomatoes (adding their juice too), onion and chopped coriander.

3 Arrange some tortilla chips on a baking sheet. Spoon a little of the salsa on to each chip, then sprinkle all over with the cheese. Pop the tray under the grill and cook for 3–5 minutes or until the cheese is bubbling and melted. Eat straight away.

• Per serving 301 kcalories, protein 8g, carbohydrate 29g, fat 18g, saturated fat 4g, fibre 4g, sugar 6g, salt 1.21g

This classic retro starter makes the most of storecupboard sauces, and the ingredients can easily be halved for a cosy dinner for two.

Classic prawn cocktail

350g/12oz unpeeled, cooked frozen prawns, defrosted
4 Little Gems, washed and trimmed
5 heaped tbsp mayonnaise
5 tbsp tomato ketchup
2 tsp Worcestershire sauce
2 tsp creamed horseradish
tiny splash of Tabasco
squeeze of fresh lemon juice
paprika, for dusting
4 tsp chives, snipped, to garnish

Takes 25 minutes • Serves 4

1 Peel all but four of the prawns (reserve these as a garnish). Break the lettuces into individual leaves and divide them evenly among four small glass bowls.
2 Sprinkle the prawns over the lettuce and season with black pepper.
3 Mix together the mayonnaise, tomato ketchup, Worcestershire sauce, horseradish and Tabasco. Season to taste with lemon juice and salt and pepper, then spoon sparingly over the prawns.
4 Dust the tops with a little paprika and sprinkle with chives. Garnish with the remaining prawns and serve immediately.

• Per serving 292 kcalories, protein 10g, carbohydrate 8g, fat 25g, saturated fat 4g, fibre 1g, sugar 8g, salt 2.23g

A really quick and healthy bagel idea that's perfect as a snack
or light lunch.

Seeded bagel tuna melt

4 mixed seed bagels
200g can tuna in spring water,
drained
1 tbsp mayonnaise
juice of 1 lemon
1 bunch spring onions, roughly
chopped
2 tomatoes, sliced
handful of grated mature Cheddar

Takes 10 minutes • Makes 4

1 Heat the grill to High. Split open the
bagels, lay them on a baking sheet, then
toast both sides until golden.
2 Meanwhile, tip the tuna into a bowl and
add the mayonnaise, lemon juice and spring
onions. Season to taste and mix well.
3 Spread the tuna mix over the bottom
half of each of the 4 bagels and top with
tomato slices. Sprinkle over the handful of
grated Cheddar, then grill for 1 minute or until
melted. Finish with the bagel tops and serve.

• Per bagel 257 kcalories, protein 17g, carbohydrate
29g, fat 9g, saturated fat 3g, fibre 2g, sugar 4g,
salt 1.28g

Falafels are cheap and easy to make, and this recipe can be easily multiplied for feeding a crowd or for serving as nibbles.

Spicy falafels

2 tbsp sunflower or vegetable oil
1 small onion, finely chopped
1 garlic clove, crushed
400g can chickpeas, drained and rinsed
1 tsp ground cumin
1 tsp ground coriander (or use more cumin)
handful of parsley leaves, chopped, or 1 tsp dried mixed herbs
1 egg, beaten

Takes 20 minutes • Makes 6

1 Heat one tablespoon of the oil in a large pan, then fry the onion and garlic over a low heat for 5 minutes or until softened.
2 Tip into a large mixing bowl with the chickpeas and spices, then mash together with a fork or potato masher until the chickpeas are totally broken down. Stir in the parsley or dried herbs, and add seasoning to taste. Add the egg, then squish the mixture together with your hands.
3 Mould the mixture into six balls, then flatten into patties. Heat the remaining oil in the pan and fry the falafels on a medium heat for 3 minutes on each side, or until golden brown and firm. Serve hot or cold with pitta bread and salad.

• Per falafel 105 kcalories, protein 5g, carbohydrate 8g, fat 6g, saturated fat 1g, fibre 2g, sugar 1g, salt 0.27g

A crafty way of using frozen peas and fish fingers to create a deliciously different dish.

Pea and pesto soup with fish-finger croûtons

500g/1lb 2oz frozen peas
4 medium potatoes, peeled and cut into cubes
1 litre/1¾ pints hot vegetable stock
300g pack fish fingers (about 10)
3 tbsp pesto

Takes 20 minutes • Serves 4

1 Tip the peas and potatoes into a large pan, then pour in the stock. Bring to the boil and simmer for 10 minutes or until the potato chunks are tender.
2 Meanwhile, grill the fish fingers as per the packet instructions, until cooked through and golden. Cut into bite-sized cubes and keep warm.
3 Take a third of the peas and potatoes out of the pan with a slotted spoon and set aside. Blend the rest of the soup until smooth, then stir in the pesto with the reserved vegetables. Heat through and serve in warm bowls with the fish-finger croûtons scattered over the top.

• Per serving 328 kcalories, protein 21g, carbohydrate 40g, fat 10g, saturated fat 3g, fibre 8g, sugar 4g, salt 1.88g

Hoisin sauce keeps well in the storecupboard and can be used to turn leftover bits of chicken or turkey into a tasty snack.

Hoisin wraps

200g/7oz cooked turkey or chicken, cut into strips
4 tbsp hoisin sauce
2 flour tortillas
½ cucumber, seeded and shredded
4 spring onions, trimmed and finely shredded
good handful of watercress

Takes 10 minutes • Makes 2

1 Heat the grill to High. Mix the turkey or chicken with half of the hoisin sauce so that it's coated, then spread over an ovenproof dish and grill until sizzling.
2 Warm the tortillas under the grill, or according to the packet instructions.
3 Spread the tortillas with the rest of the hoisin sauce, add the turkey or chicken with the cucumber, onions and watercress, and wrap up the whole lot. Cut in half and enjoy while still warm.

• Per wrap 302 kcalories, protein 33g, carbohydrate 31g, fat 6g, saturated fat 1g, fibre 2g, sugar 12g, salt 1.81g

For a vegetarian version, swap the chipolatas for veggie sausages, omit the bacon and add more mushrooms.

One-pan English breakfast

4 good-quality pork chipolatas
4 rashers smoked back bacon
140g/5oz button mushrooms
6 eggs, beaten
8 cherry tomatoes, halved
handful of grated cheese (optional)
1 tbsp snipped chives

Takes 20 minutes • Serves 4

1 Heat the grill to High. Heat a medium non-stick frying pan, add the chipolatas and fry for 3 minutes. Add the bacon and cook, turning occasionally, until it starts to crisp – about 5 minutes more. Tip in the mushrooms and continue to cook for a further 3–5 minutes. Drain off any excess fat and move the ingredients around the pan so they are evenly spread out.
2 Season the eggs, then add them to the pan, swirling them to fill the spaces. Gently move the egg around with a fork for 2 minutes over a low–medium heat until it is beginning to set.
3 Scatter over the tomatoes, cheese, if using, and chives, then grill for 2 minutes until set. Cut into wedges and serve with your favourite sauces.

• Per serving 349 kcalories, protein 25g, carbohydrate 4g, fat 26g, saturated fat 8g, fibre 1g, sugar 2g, salt 2.27g

Needing just five ingredients and only 5 minutes to cook, this omelette is the perfect dish to cook with children. You can easily multiply the ingredients if you want to feed the whole family.

Omelette in five

2 eggs
1 tsp butter
1 tbsp grated cheese
2 cherry tomatoes, halved
1 spring onion, sliced
green salad, to serve

Takes 10 minutes • Serves 1

1 Break the eggs into a bowl and whisk gently with a fork until the white and the yolk are combined.

2 Heat a small frying pan over a medium heat, then add the butter. When the butter has melted and is starting to sizzle, pour in the beaten eggs. Using a spatula, pull the cooked eggs from around the outside of the pan into the middle to allow the runny eggs to cook evenly. Once the eggs are almost set, sprinkle the cheese, tomatoes and spring onion over.

3 Fold one half of the omelette over the other, using a spatula (tilting the pan often helps, too). Lift the omelette on to a plate and serve straight away with a crispy salad.

• Per serving 266 kcalories, protein 18g, carbohydrate 1g, fat 21g, saturated fat 8g, fibre none, sugar 1g, salt 0.7g

This quick curry is packed with healthy vegetables and is a feast for vegetarians and non-vegetarians alike.

Egg curry

3 eggs
1 onion, finely sliced
1 tbsp vegetable oil
2 tbsp korma curry paste
175g/6oz green beans, trimmed and halved
175g/6oz young spinach leaves
175g/6oz cherry tomatoes
100ml/3fl oz reduced-fat coconut milk
naan or pitta bread, to serve

Takes 30 minutes • Serves 2

1 Boil the eggs for 8 minutes, then cool under cold running water before peeling off the shells.
2 Fry the onion in the oil for about 5 minutes or until softened and lightly coloured, then stir in the curry paste and beans. Add 200ml/7fl oz water, then cover and cook for 5 minutes. Add the spinach, tomatoes and coconut milk, then bring to a simmer, stirring until the spinach is just wilted.
3 Spoon on to two plates, then halve the eggs and sit them on top. Serve with toasted naan or pitta breads.

• Per serving 351 kcalories, protein 18g, carbohydrate 14g, fat 26g, saturated fat 8g, fibre 6g, sugar 10g, salt 1.38g

Use up whatever you have in the fridge for this speedy supper dish – mushrooms, bacon, red pepper, frozen peas and green beans all work well with the potatoes and eggs.

Anytime eggs

1 tbsp olive oil
2–3 cooked potatoes, sliced
handful of cherry tomatoes, halved
2 spring onions, sliced
1 egg
a few basil leaves, to garnish

Takes 20 minutes • Serves 1

1 Heat the oil in a frying pan, throw in the potato slices and fry on both sides until golden brown. Scatter over the tomatoes and spring onions and fry for about 1 minute more until softened. Season with a little salt and generously with pepper, then push the potatoes to the sides to make a space in the pan.
2 Gently break the egg into the space and fry until cooked to your liking. Scatter over the basil leaves and serve.

• Per serving 305 kcalories, protein 11g, carbohydrate 27g, fat 18g, saturated fat 3g, fibre 2g, sugar 2g, salt 0.59g

This deluxe omelette is so good it's ideal for sharing with someone special.

Smoked salmon and mascarpone tortilla

400g/14oz (about 2 large) potatoes, cut into thick slices
1 small bunch dill, stalks removed
6 eggs
2 tbsp mascarpone or full-fat soft cheese
1 tbsp sunflower oil
100g/4oz frozen peas
125g pack smoked salmon, thickly sliced
green salad, to serve

Takes 20 minutes • Serves 2

1 Boil the potato slices for about 10 minutes or until just tender, then drain. Roughly chop the dill leaves and beat them into the eggs, along with one tablespoon of mascarpone or soft cheese. Season to taste.

2 Heat the oil in a small frying pan (around 20cm/8in diameter is ideal), then add the cooked potatoes, frozen peas and the egg mixture. Leave to set on a low heat for about 7 minutes, pushing the mixture around the pan every so often so that it cooks evenly.

3 Heat the grill to High. Once the tortilla is firm underneath, but still a little wobbly on top, drape the salmon slices over the top and dot with the remaining cheese. Season with black pepper, then flash under the grill until just set. Serve with a green salad.

• Per serving 684 kcalories, protein 43g, carbohydrate 40g, fat 40g, saturated fat 12g, fibre 5g, sugar 3g, salt 0.79g

This veggie classic stands the test of time and is still a real showstopper.

Classic cheese soufflé

50g/2oz butter, plus extra for greasing
25g/1oz breadcrumbs
50g/2oz plain flour
1 tsp mustard powder
300ml/½ pint milk
4 eggs
100g/4oz extra-strong Cheddar, grated

Takes 40 minutes, plus cooling
Serves 4

1 Preheat the oven to 200°C/fan 180°C/gas 6. Place a baking sheet on the middle shelf. Butter a 15cm/6in soufflé dish and sprinkle in the breadcrumbs.
2 Melt the butter in a pan. Stir in the flour and mustard powder. Gradually stir in the milk, mixing thoroughly before adding more. Stir continuously until the liquid thickens, then transfer to a bowl. Separate the eggs, placing the whites in a clean bowl. Stir the yolks into the sauce with the Cheddar.
4 Whisk the egg whites until peaks form. With a metal spoon, gently stir the whipped whites into the white sauce.
5 Spoon the mixture into the prepared soufflé dish. Run a cutlery knife around the edge to create a 'top hat' effect. Place on the baking sheet and bake for 25–30 minutes or until the top is golden, risen and has a slight wobble. Serve immediately.

• Per serving 402 kcalories, protein 19g, carbohydrate 18g, fat 29g, saturated fat 15g, fibre 1g, sugar 4g, salt 1.02g

By separating the eggs and whisking the whites, this recipe gives you an altogether lighter omelette.

Summer soufflé omelette

4 eggs
1 tbsp grated Parmesan
small handful of basil leaves, finely shredded
1 tbsp olive oil
50g/2oz goat's cheese, broken into chunks
4 cherry tomatoes, halved

Takes 15 minutes • Serves 2

1 Heat the grill to High. Crack the eggs, then separate the yolks from the whites into two bowls. Tip the Parmesan and most of the basil in with the yolks and season. Whisk the whites vigorously for about a minute or until light and fluffy, then, using the same whisk, beat the yolks with the Parmesan and basil. Finally, whisk the yolk mix into the egg whites.
2 Heat the oil in a small frying pan and tip in the egg mix. Leave to cook for a minute, then scatter over the goat's cheese and tomatoes.
3 Place the pan under the grill for 5 minutes or until puffed up, golden and set with only the slightest wobble. Scatter over the remaining basil leaves, then serve the soufflé omelette straight from the pan with a salad on the side.

• Per serving 302 kcalories, protein 20g, carbohydrate 1g, fat 24g, saturated fat 8g, fibre none, sugar 2g, salt 0.81g

Easy, cheap and tasty – the perfect dish for a speedy midweek meal.

Courgette, potato and mint frittata

2 medium potatoes, sliced
1 tbsp olive oil
1 medium courgettes, sliced
4 eggs
handful of mint leaves, roughly chopped
100g/4oz Cheddar

Takes 30 minutes • Serves 2

1 Boil the potatoes for 6 minutes or until just cooked, then drain and set aside. Heat the oil in a large, deep ovenproof frying pan and fry the courgettes for 4–5 minutes until golden. Tip in the potatoes and fry for 1 minute with the courgettes.

2 Heat the grill to High. In a bowl, beat together the eggs and mint, then season. Pour into the frying pan and stir briefly. Cook for 5 minutes over a low heat.

3 Crumble over the cheese and put the pan under the grill for 5 minutes or until the eggs are just set and the cheese has browned. Serve cut into wedges.

• Per serving 546 kcalories, protein 32g, carbohydrate 23g, fat 37g, saturated fat 15g, fibre 2g, sugar 2g, salt 1.37g

For a comforting supper, try cooking egg and chips in one pan.

Oven egg and chips

450g/1lb floury potatoes, such as
King Edward potatoes or
Maris Piper
2 garlic cloves, sliced
4 fresh rosemary sprigs or 1 tsp
dried
2 tbsp olive oil
2 eggs

Takes 1 hour • Serves 2

1 Preheat the oven to 220°C/fan 200°C/ gas 7. Without peeling, cut the potatoes into thick chips. Tip them into a roasting tin (non-stick is best) and scatter over the garlic. Strip the rosemary leaves from the sprigs and sprinkle them, or the dried rosemary, over too. Drizzle with the oil, season well, then toss the chips to coat them in the oil and flavourings.

2 Oven-roast the chips for 35–40 minutes or until just cooked and golden, shaking the tin halfway through.

3 Make two gaps between the chips and break an egg into each. Return to the oven for 3–5 minutes or until the eggs are cooked to your liking.

• Per serving 348 kcalories, protein 11g, carbohydrate 40g, fat 17g, saturated fat 3g, fibre 3g, sugar none, salt 0.22g

These tasty, individual tarts use modern, popular ingredients that you can keep in the fridge, freezer and storecupboard.

Chorizo, egg and pepper tarts

375g pack ready-rolled puff pastry
2 tsp sun-dried tomato paste
4 handfuls of frozen roasted peppers
(or from a jar, drained)
8 slices chorizo sausage, torn
4 eggs

Takes 25 minutes • Makes 4

1 Preheat the oven to 220°C/fan 200°C/gas 7. Cut the unrolled pastry into four rectangles. Etch a border inside each one, a finger's width from the edge. Lift the pastry on to a baking sheet. Spread the tomato paste over the inside of the pastry frames. Spread the peppers over the middle of the tarts and bake for 10 minutes (pastry will be light golden and just risen at this point). Turn the oven down to 180°C/fan 160°C/gas 4.
2 Tuck the chorizo among the peppers and break an egg into the middle of each tart. Grind over some black pepper and return to the oven for 5 minutes, or until the white is set and the egg yolk just runny. If you prefer a really runny yolk, bake the tarts with the chorizo on top for 5 minutes, then top with a fried or poached egg instead.

• Per tart 485 kcalories, protein 15g, carbohydrate 37g, fat 32g, saturated fat 11g, fibre 1g, sugar 3g, salt 1.54g

This salad makes a simple supper, and you can pack up any leftovers in a lunchbox for the next day.

Hot pasta salad

300g/10oz penne
4 tbsp mayonnaise
juice of 1 lemon
200g can tuna in olive oil
2 red peppers, seeded and thinly sliced
1 red onion, halved and finely sliced
large handful of rocket leaves, to garnish

Takes 20 minutes • Serves 4

1 Cook the pasta according to the packet instructions. Meanwhile, tip the mayonnaise, lemon juice and one tablespoon of the tuna oil into a large bowl and mix. Drain the rest of the oil from the tuna, then flake the fish into the bowl and mix well.

2 Drain the pasta and toss it with the mayonnaise mixture, peppers and onions. Scatter over the rocket just before serving.

• Per serving 476 kcalories, protein 21g, carbohydrate 64g, fat 17g, saturated fat 3g, fibre 4g, sugar 8g, salt 0.5g

A fast family meal that uses just five ingredients, making it perfect for a manic midweek supper.

Pea, prawn and lemon linguine

350g/12oz linguine
200g/7oz frozen peas, defrosted
300g/10oz frozen cooked peeled prawns, defrosted
zest and juice of 1 lemon
100ml/3½fl oz double cream

Takes 15 minutes, plus defrosting
Serves 4

1 Cook the pasta according to the packet instructions. Meanwhile, heat a non-stick pan, then gently cook the peas, prawns, lemon zest and juice for 3–4 minutes or until the prawns are hot and the peas are tender.
2 Season the prawns and peas well, stir in the cream and two tablespoons of the pasta water, then allow to bubble for 1 minute. Drain the linguine and return to the pan with the sauce, tossing it well to coat. Serve in individual bowls.

• Per serving 536 kcalories, protein 31g, carbohydrate 72g, fat 16g, saturated fat 8g, fibre 5g, sugar 4g, salt 1.38g

To make this even quicker, you can use a large jar of bought tomato and herb pasta sauce instead of making your own.

Ham and olive lasagne

250g pack fresh lasagne sheets
1 tbsp oil
1 fat garlic clove, crushed
2 x 400g cans chopped tomatoes with herbs
8 slices ham
generous handful of green olives
2 eggs
150g carton mild natural yogurt
50g/2oz Cheddar, grated, plus a handful extra for the top

Takes 25 minutes • Serves 4

1 Preheat the oven to 190°C/fan 170°C/gas 5. Put the lasagne sheets into a bowl and pour over just-boiled water. Leave to soak for 5 minutes, then drain.

2 Heat the oil in an ovenproof frying pan. Fry the garlic for 1 minute. Add the tomatoes, then simmer for 5 minutes to reduce a little. Season to taste, then tip into a bowl.

3 Layer the pasta sheets, ham (keep this in slices), tomato sauce and olives in the frying pan, making sure you have a few olives and some sauce on the top.

4 Beat the eggs, yogurt and most of the cheese together in a jug, season with salt and pepper, then pour over the pasta. Top with extra cheese and black pepper, then bake for 15 minutes or until the cheese is golden and the topping is set.

• Per serving 346 kcalories, protein 25g, carbohydrate 28g, fat 16g, saturated fat 5g, fibre 3g, sugar 7g, salt 2.52g

To give this dish a little extra flavour, use grilled artichokes – you can find these in jars in most good supermarkets or delis.

Quick springtime pasta

1 tbsp olive oil
1 garlic clove, crushed
400g can chopped tomatoes
handful of basil leaves, chopped
400g/14oz spaghetti
290g jar artichoke hearts, cut into bite-sized pieces
handful of freshly grated Parmesan
handful of parsley, chopped

Takes 25 minutes • Serves 4

1 Heat the olive oil in a large pan. Tip in the garlic and cook for 1 minute or until lightly coloured. Pour in the chopped tomatoes, then stir in the basil. Bring to the boil, then turn down the heat and leave to simmer gently for 10 minutes. Meanwhile, boil the spaghetti according to the packet instructions.

2 Drain the spaghetti, reserving a little of the cooking water, then return to the pan. Add the artichokes to the tomato sauce and heat through, then pour over the spaghetti. Stir in a little Parmesan, most of the chopped parsley and a splash of the cooking water, if the sauce looks dry. Serve immediately with the remaining Parmesan and parsley sprinkled over.

• Per serving 494 kcalories, protein 16g, carbohydrate 79g, fat 15g, saturated fat 3g, fibre 5g, sugar 6g, salt 1.14g

This is a fresh, seasonal and colourful dish that's really easy to prepare.

Roasted veg pasta with Cheshire pesto

1 large bunch basil, leaves picked off but keep the stalks
2 tbsp olive oil
2 garlic cloves
250g bundle asparagus, trimmed
250g pack cooked beetroot (not in vinegar)
400g/14oz pappardelle, or your favourite long pasta
100g/4oz sharp Cheshire cheese, crumbled
2 tbsp pine nuts, toasted

Takes 25 minutes • Serves 4

1 Preheat the oven to 220°C/fan 200°C/gas 7. Put the basil stalks and most of the leaves into a food processor. Add the oil and garlic plus a splash of water, then whiz to a rough paste. Put the asparagus at one end of a roasting tin and the beetroot at the other. Season well, then rub with about one tablespoon of the basil mix. Roast for 7–10 minutes or until the asparagus starts to caramelize and is cooked, but still firm.
2 Meanwhile, boil the pasta according to the packet instructions. Add half the cheese to the basil mix and whiz again to make a cheesey pesto. Season to taste. Drain the pasta, then toss with the pesto, remaining cheese, pine nuts and roasted vegetables. Serve sprinkled with the remaining basil leaves.

• Per serving 571 kcalories, protein 22g, carbohydrate 84g, fat 19g, saturated fat 6g, fibre 5g, sugar 9g, salt 0.55g

A low-fat but satisfying supper that you can throw together in minutes.

Spaghetti with tomato, chilli and tuna salsa

350g/12oz spaghetti
1 small red onion
500g/1lb 2oz fresh tomatoes
2 tbsp olive oil
1 red chilli
140g can tuna in brine, drained

Takes 20 minutes • Serves 4

1 Cook the spaghetti in plenty of boiling, salted water according to the packet instructions.
2 Meanwhile, finely chop the onion and tomatoes and put them in a large pan along with the oil. Halve, seed and finely chop the chilli, then add to the pan. Gently heat through for a few minutes, stirring well.
3 Drain the pasta and add to the sauce, then break up the tuna and add to the pan. Season to taste, then toss well and serve in bowls.

• Per serving 404 kcalories, protein 18g, carbohydrate 70g, fat 8g, saturated fat 1g, fibre 4g, sugar 8g, salt 0.52g

You can add your own flavours to this pesto recipe if you have other ingredients to hand, such as watercress and walnuts, or pine nuts and rocket.

Pasta with parsley and hazelnut pesto

350g/12oz tagliatelle
80g pack flat-leaf parsley
100g/4oz toasted hazelnuts
50g/2oz Parmesan, grated
zest and juice of 1 lemon
100ml/3½fl oz olive oil

Takes 20 minutes • Serves 4

1 Cook the pasta in salted, boiling water according to the packet instructions.
2 Put the parsley, hazelnuts, Parmesan and lemon zest and juice into a food processor and whiz to a rough paste. With the motor still running, gradually drizzle in the olive oil. Season, if you like, with salt and pepper.
3 Drain the pasta well, return it to the pan and stir in the pesto so that all the pasta is coated. Divide the pasta among bowls and serve.

• Per serving 727 kcalories, protein 19g, carbohydrate 70g, fat 43g, saturated fat 7g, fibre 5g, sugar 3g, salt 0.27g

This classic pasta dish is an all-time favourite that's perfect for pleasing a crowd.

Classic spaghetti carbonara

600g/1lb 5oz spaghetti
2 tbsp vegetable oil
300g/10oz rindless rashers smoked back bacon or pancetta, cut into thin strips
1 tsp freshly ground black pepper
5 eggs
100ml/3½fl oz single cream
100g/4oz grated Parmesan, plus extra to serve
handful of flat-leaf parsley, chopped

Takes 25 minutes • Serves 6

1 Bring a large pan of water to the boil, then cook the pasta according to the packet instructions.
2 While the pasta is cooking, heat a large frying pan and add the oil. Throw in the bacon and sizzle for 3 minutes, shaking the pan well every minute or so. When the bacon is crisp, add the black pepper. Crack the eggs into a bowl and beat with a fork. Stir the cream into the eggs and set aside.
3 Drain the pasta. Return to the pan over a low heat and add the bacon and any fat from the frying pan. Toss well, keeping it on the heat. Cook for 1 minute, then add the egg mixture and the Parmesan, and cook for 1 minute more or until the egg is just setting. Add the chopped parsley and serve straight away with grated Parmesan.

• Per serving 679 kcalories, protein 33g, carbohydrate 75g, fat 29g, saturated fat 11g, fibre 3g, sugar 4g, salt 2.48g

A heart-healthy meal that's on the table in just 20 minutes.

Smoked trout and pea pasta

175g/6oz fusilli or other short pasta
100g/4oz frozen peas
125g pack smoked trout fillets
3 rounded tbsp 0% Greek yogurt
2 rounded tsp horseradish sauce

Takes 20 minutes • Serves 4

1 Cook the pasta in a large pan of boiling, salted water according to the packet instructions, adding the peas for the last 3 minutes of the cooking time.
2 Meanwhile, flake the trout and set aside, then mix the yogurt with the horseradish and season with a little salt and pepper.
3 Drain the pasta, then return to the pan and stir in the trout and yogurt mixture, letting the heat of the pasta warm the sauce through. This dish is delicious served with a crisp green salad.

• Per serving 445 kcalories, protein 30g, carbohydrate 74g, fat 6g, saturated fat 1g, fibre 5g, sugar 4g, salt 1.78g

If you're planning to cook this dish when you're short of time, speed things up a bit by buying ready-trimmed and sliced runner beans.

Prawn, sweetcorn and runner bean pasta

400g/14oz pasta tubes (such as penne)
200g fresh or frozen runner beans, trimmed and sliced
400g fresh or frozen sweetcorn,
5 tbsp fromage frais
5 tbsp coriander pesto
200g bag cooked peeled prawns, defrosted if frozen
coriander leaves, to serve (optional)

Takes 15 minutes plus defrosting
Serves 4

1 Cook the pasta according to the packet instructions. Tip in the runner beans and sweetcorn for the final 4 minutes of the pasta cooking time. Drain, remove from the pan and set aside.

2 Mix the fromage frais and pesto together, then pour into the same saucepan, along with the prawns. Warm through briefly over a low heat, then tip in the pasta and veg. Take off the heat, toss together and sprinkle with coriander, if using.

• Per serving 552 kcalories, protein 30g, carbohydrate 92g, fat 10g, saturated fat 3g, fibre 5g, sugar 9g, salt 2.14g

This recipe creates a luxuriously creamy pasta dish, while still keeping the ingredients to a minimum.

Creamy mushroom spaghetti

400g/14oz spaghetti
6 rashers rindless streaky bacon, cut into strips
250g pack chestnut or button mushrooms, sliced
200g bag baby spinach
100g/4oz Gorgonzola or creamy blue cheese, crumbled

Takes 25 minutes • Serves 4

1 Bring a large pan of water to the boil, then cook the spaghetti according to the packet instructions.
2 Meanwhile, fry the bacon in a large frying pan for 5 minutes or until starting to crisp. Tip in the mushrooms, then fry for 3 minutes or until cooked.
3 Drain the pasta and tip into the frying pan along with the spinach and cheese. Toss everything together over a low heat until the spinach has wilted and the cheese melted. Serve in individual bowls.

• Per serving 505 kcalories, protein 24g, carbohydrate 75g, fat 14g, saturated fat 7g, fibre 5g, sugar 4g, salt 1.80g

A really quick idea for a satisfying, yet healthy lunch or supper. The ingredients can easily be multiplied to feed a crowd.

Instant meatballs with penne

200g/7oz penne
3 fat sausages
1 tbsp olive oil
250g bag spinach
3 tbsp pine nuts, toasted
50g/2oz Parmesan, grated

Takes 25 minutes • Serves 2

1 Cook the pasta according to the packet instructions. Meanwhile, squeeze the sausages from their skins, then roughly break up the meat into twelve pieces. Roll each of these pieces into a ball.

2 Heat the oil in a large frying pan, add the sausage balls, then cook over a medium heat until golden, about 5 minutes. Pile the spinach on top of the sausage balls and cook, stirring frequently, for 2–3 minutes or until completely wilted. Season with a little salt and plenty of ground black pepper, then toss in the toasted pine nuts.

3 Drain the pasta and add it to the sausages and spinach, then toss well, adding half the Parmesan. Serve spooned into individual serving bowls with the rest of the Parmesan scattered on top.

• Per serving 964 kcalories, protein 39g, carbohydrate 88g, fat 53g, saturated fat 16g, fibre 7g, sugar 8g, salt 3.14g

Try this new way to serve couscous for a tasty midweek meal.

Couscous fritters with feta

175g/6oz couscous
200ml/7fl oz hot vegetable stock
1 egg, beaten
3 tbsp natural yogurt
85g/3oz feta, cut into
1cm/½in cubes
50g/2oz SunBlush tomatoes,
finely chopped
3 spring onions, finely chopped
2 tbsp sunflower oil or vegetable oil
green salad and chutney, to serve

Takes 20 minutes • Makes 4

1 Tip the couscous into a large heatproof bowl, pour over the hot stock, then cover with cling film. Leave to stand for 5 minutes or until the couscous has absorbed the stock and the grains are soft. Add the egg and yogurt and mix well. Season, then fold through the cheese, tomatoes and spring onions.

2 Divide the mixture into four and shape into burgers. Heat the oil in a non-stick frying pan, then cook the fritters over a medium heat for 3 minutes on each side or until golden. Serve with a green salad and a spoonful of your favourite chutney.

• Per fritter 510 kcalories, protein 19g, carbohydrate 51g, fat 27g, saturated fat 8g, fibre 1g, sugar 7g, salt 2.6g

Using straight-to-wok noodles means you will have supper on the table in just 10 minutes.

Sesame noodles with tofu

250g pack firm tofu, drained
2 tbsp reduced-salt soy sauce, plus extra to serve (optional)
2 teaspoons sesame oil, plus extra to serve (optional)
300g/10oz green veg
1 garlic clove, sliced
small knob of fresh root ginger, peeled and shredded
300g pack straight-to-wok egg noodles (or use 2 sheets medium dried egg noodles and follow packet instructions)
1 tbsp sesame seeds

Takes 10 minutes • Serves 2

1 Cut the tofu into twelve pieces and mix with one tablespoon of soy sauce and one teaspoon of sesame oil. Heat the remaining oil in a wok, then stir fry the vegetables, garlic and ginger for 2 minutes or until the vegetables are starting to wilt. Drizzle with two tablespoons of water, then stir fry for another minute.

2 Add the noodles, sesame seeds and soy sauce from the marinated tofu, then stir fry for 2 minutes. Now add the tofu, splash over the remaining soy sauce, then cover with a lid or baking sheet. Leave for 1 minute so that the tofu heats through, then gently mix into the rest of the stir fry.

3 Lift the noodles and tofu into bowls and splash over a little more soy sauce and sesame oil to serve, if you like.

• Per serving 531 kcalories, protein 27g, carbohydrate 74g, fat 17g, saturated fat 2g, fibre 5g, sugar 6g, salt 3.35g

This quick, tasty low-fat dish uses many storecupboard basics.

Quick beef and broccoli noodles

3 blocks egg noodles
1 head broccoli, cut into small florets
1 tbsp sesame oil
400g pack beef stir-fry strips
1 spring onion, sliced, to garnish

FOR THE SAUCE
3 tbsp low-salt soy sauce
2 tbsp oyster sauce (not oyster stir-fry sauce)
1 tbsp tomato ketchup
2 garlic cloves, crushed
1 thumb-sized knob fresh root ginger, peeled and finely grated
1 tbsp white wine vinegar

Takes 20 minutes • Serves 4

1 Start by making up the sauce. Mix all the ingredients together in a small bowl until completely combined.
2 Boil the noodles according to the packet instructions. A minute before they are ready, tip in the broccoli.
3 Meanwhile, heat the oil in a wok until very hot, then stir fry the beef for 2–3 minutes or until well browned. Tip in the sauce, give it a stir, let it simmer for a moment, then turn off the heat. Drain the noodles and broccoli, stir into the beef and serve straight away, scattered with the sliced spring onion.

Per serving 352 kcalories, protein 33g, carbohydrate 39g, fat 9g, saturated fat 2g, fibre 4g, sugar 5g, salt 3g

This simple, healthy recipe is packed with flavour and is a great way to boost your iron intake.

Couscous and fish in a bag

1 lemon
100g/4oz couscous
25g/1oz pine nuts, toasted
1 small courgette, thinly sliced
small handful of dill, leaves only, chopped
150ml/¼ pint strong vegetable stock
1 haddock fillet or other white fish

Takes 35 minutes • Serves 1

1 Preheat the oven to 180°C/fan 160°C/gas 4. Fold a large sheet of foil or non-stick baking paper in half and tightly fold one side to seal. Grate the lemon and mix the zest into the couscous, pine nuts, courgette and dill. Season well, then tip into the open 'bag'. Cut the lemon in half, then cut 2 thin slices from one half. Juice the other half and add the juice to the stock.
2 Lay the haddock on top of the couscous, top with the lemon slices, then carefully pour over the lemony stock. Fold the remaining open sides tightly to seal. Bake for 20–25 minutes, depending on how thick your fish is, until the fish is cooked and couscous is fluffy.

• Per serving 552 kcalories, protein 41g, carbohydrate 57g, fat 20g, saturated fat 23g, fibre 2.1g, sugar 6g, salt 0.46g

This easy supper is also delicious with a large handful of flaked smoked mackerel gently mixed into the rice.

Poached egg with spicy rice

1 tsp oil
½ onion, chopped
½ green pepper, seeded and sliced
1 x 250g pouch microwave pilau basmati rice
50g/2oz frozen peas
1 tsp medium curry powder
1 egg

Takes 20 minutes • Serves 1

1 Heat the oil in a non-stick frying pan. Fry the onion and pepper for 5–8 minutes or until soft and beginning to brown. Tip in the rice, frozen peas, curry powder and 200ml/7fl oz water, stir well, then simmer gently for 10 minutes.
2 Bring a small pan of water to the boil and, when the rice is almost ready, poach the egg. Serve the rice with the egg on top.

• Per serving 711 kcalories, protein 50g, carbohydrate 62g, fat 31g, saturated fat 4g, fibre 6g, sugar 7g, salt 0.25g

A great midweek one-pot with a lovely coconut flavour.

Oven-baked Thai chicken rice

1 tbsp vegetable oil
1 onion, chopped
400g pack mini chicken fillets
4 tbsp Thai green curry paste (or use less for a milder taste)
250g/8oz basmati and wild rice mix, rinsed
2 red peppers, seeded and cut into wedges
finely grated zest and juice of 1 lime
400g reduced-fat coconut milk
handful of coriander leaves, to serve

Takes 35 minutes • Serves 4

1 Preheat the oven to 200°C/fan 180°C/gas 6. Heat the oil in a shallow ovenproof casserole dish, then soften the onion for 5 minutes. Add the chicken and curry paste, then cook for 3 minutes, stirring to coat.
2 Tip in the rice and peppers, then stir in the lime zest and juice, coconut milk and 250ml/8fl oz boiling water. Bring to the boil, then pop the lid on and bake for 20 minutes until the rice is fluffy. Scatter with coriander before serving.

• Per serving 510 kcalories, protein 32g, carbohydrate 59g, fat 18g, saturated fat 10g, fibre 2g, sugar 8g, salt 1.02g

A classic recipe made using a cheat's method. Simply pop it in the microwave for speedy, delicious results.

Microwave risotto primavera

350g/12oz risotto rice
175ml/6fl oz white wine
850ml/1½ pints hot vegetable stock
500g/1lb 2oz frozen peas and beans mix
100g/4oz pack asparagus tips
100g/4oz soft goat's cheese
handful of mint leaves, roughly torn

Takes 25 minutes • Serves 4

1 Measure the rice into a large microwaveable bowl, then pour in the wine and a third of the stock. Cover with cling film, then microwave on High for 10 minutes. Stir the rice, then add another third of the stock, re-cover and microwave again for 3 minutes.
2 Stir the rice again, then add the frozen veg, asparagus and the rest of the stock. Re-cover and microwave for 7 minutes. Stir in the cheese and mint, then leave the risotto to stand for 2 minutes before serving.

• Per serving 461 kcalories, protein 19g, carbohydrate 84g, fat 6g, saturated fat 3g, fibre 9g, sugar 7g, salt 0.6g

With a few crafty kitchen tricks you'll have this Spanish classic on the table in no time.

Easiest-ever paella

1 tbsp olive oil
1 leek or onion, sliced
110g pack chorizo sausage, chopped
1 tsp tumeric
300g/10oz long grain rice
1 litre/1¾ pints hot fish or chicken stock
200g/7oz frozen peas
400g/14oz frozen seafood mix, defrosted
lemon wedges, to serve

Takes 30 minutes, plus defrosting
Serves 4

1 Heat the oil in a deep frying pan, then soften the leek or onion for 5 minutes without browning. Add the chorizo and fry until it releases its oils. Stir in the turmeric and rice until coated by the oils, then pour in the stock. Bring to the boil, then simmer for 15 minutes, stirring occasionally.
2 Tip in the peas for the last 5 minutes of cooking time, then stir in the seafood to heat through in the final 1–2 minutes, or until the rice is cooked. Check for seasoning and serve immediately with lemon wedges.

• Per serving 518 kcalories, protein 32g, carbohydrate 75g, fat 12g, saturated fat 0.4g, fibre 5g, sugar 5g, salt 1.29g

Noodles and tofu make this recipe a filling supper, while the chilli and peanuts give it flavour.

Asian-style tofu and cucumber noodles

2 tbsp soy sauce
knob of fresh root ginger, peeled and shredded
1 lime, ½ juiced, ½ cut into wedges
250g pack firm tofu, drained
2 sheets medium egg noodles
1 tsp vegetable or sunflower oil
1 red chilli, seeded and finely sliced
½ cucumber, peeled into ribbons
1 tbsp toasted peanuts, crushed

Takes 20 minutes • Serves 4

1 Mix the soy sauce, ginger and lime juice in a dish, then add the tofu. Leave to marinate for 5 minutes, turning once. Boil the noodles for 4 minutes, or according to the packet instructions, then drain and cool.

2 Dry the tofu on kitchen paper, reserving the marinade. Heat the oil in a non-stick frying pan, then fry the tofu for 3 minutes on each side until golden. Cut into cubes.

3 To serve, mix the noodles, chilli, cucumber, tofu and the marinade in a bowl. Toss, then serve with lime wedges and peanuts.

• Per serving 179 kcalories, protein 10g, carbohydrate 24g, fat 6g, saturated fat 1g, fibre 1g, sugar 2g, salt 1.8g

This no-cook salad is fresh and light with a citrus zing that will awaken the tastebuds at the end of a long day.

Prawn rice-noodle salad

250g pack thin rice noodles
1 ripe mango
200g/7oz peeled prawns
1 bunch spring onions, sliced
20g pack coriander, chopped

FOR THE DRESSING
2 rounded tbsp crunchy peanut butter
1 tbsp light muscovado sugar
good pinch of chilli powder
juice of 2 limes

Takes 20 minutes • Serves 4

1 Bring a full kettle to the boil and pour the boiling water over the noodles. Leave them to stand for 4 minutes, then drain and cool under cold running water. Drain well. Halve the mango either side of the stone, then peel each half and chop the flesh. Mix the chopped mango with the noodles, prawns, spring onions and coriander.
2 For the dressing, mix together the peanut butter, sugar and chilli powder, then stir in the lime juice until everything is completely combined. Drizzle the dressing over the salad and toss well, to serve.

• Per serving 421 kcalories, protein 20g, carbohydrate 72g, fat 8g, saturated fat 1g, fibre 5g, sugar 17g, salt 1.04g

Here's a great salad to feed a crowd at a barbecue or, as it sits well, to take along to a picnic.

Lemony rice and peas

300g/10oz brown basmati rice
75ml/2½fl oz olive oil
200g/7oz frozen peas
410g can lentils, drained and rinsed
410g can chickpeas, drained and rinsed
juice of 2 lemons
2 bunches spring onions, finely sliced
1 large bunch coriander, chopped, to serve

Takes 35 minutes • Serves 10

1 Cook the rice in a large pan of boiling water for about 15 minutes, drain and drizzle with a little of the olive oil, then leave to cool.
2 Boil a kettle and pour the water over the peas in a small bowl. Leave them to defrost, then drain. In a large bowl, mix the rice with the peas, lentils, chickpeas, remaining olive oil, lemon juice and the spring onions. Season to taste. The rice salad can now be kept in the fridge for up to 2 days. Remove from the fridge about 30 minutes before serving, then stir through the coriander.

• Per serving 229 kcalories, protein 7g, carbohydrate 32g, fat 9g, saturated fat 1g, fibre 4g, sugar 2g, salt 0.61g

This comforting risotto is a delicious way to include oily fish in a simple midweek supper.

Smoked mackerel risotto

1 tbsp butter
1 onion, finely chopped
250g/9oz risotto rice
100ml/3½fl oz white wine
1 litre/1¾ pints hot vegetable stock
240g pack smoked mackerel
2 spring onions, sliced
100g bag spinach

Takes 25 minutes • Serves 4

1 Heat the butter in a large frying pan. Tip in the onion, then fry gently for 5 minutes until softened. Stir in the rice and mix until coated in the butter, then pour in the wine and let it bubble until it has almost all disappeared.
2 Pour in half the stock, give it a good stir, then leave to gently cook for 10 minutes. Add half of the remaining stock, stir again and cook for 5 minutes more. Keep adding the stock and cooking until the rice is tender.
3 Peel the skin off the mackerel, scrape away any dark brown flesh, then flake. Stir into the rice with the spring onions and spinach, then cook just until the spinach has wilted slightly. Serve straight away.

• Per serving 492 kcalories, protein 18g, carbohydrate 23g, fat 7g, saturated fat 5g, fibre 3g, sugar 5g, salt 1.62g

This quick risotto can easily be made into a vegetarian dish by leaving out the bacon and adding two or three large grilled mushrooms instead.

Leek and sage risotto with crispy bacon

1 tbsp olive oil
2 leeks, sliced
4 sage leaves, shredded, or a pinch of dried
85g/3oz risotto rice
small glass white wine
200ml/7fl oz hot vegetable stock
2–3 rashers rindless streaky bacon
3 tbsp Parmesan, grated

Takes 30 minutes • Serves 1

1 Heat the oil in a pan, add the leeks and sage and fry for 2 minutes or until the leeks are starting to soften. Stir in the rice and cook for 1 minute, stirring. Add the wine and stock and bring to the boil. Reduce the heat, cover and simmer for 10–12 minutes or until the rice is tender.

2 Meanwhile, grill the bacon until golden and crisp. Remove the rice from the heat, then stir in two tablespoons of the Parmesan and some freshly ground pepper. Spoon on to a plate, sprinkle with the remaining Parmesan and top with the bacon.

• Per serving 685 kcalories, protein 27g, carbohydrate 81g, fat 27g, saturated fat 9g, fibre 8g, sugar 13g, salt 1.65g

There's no need to get a take-away – get some friends round instead to enjoy this simple yet tasty biryani.

Quick lamb biryani

1 tbsp balti curry paste
500g/1lb 2oz lean lamb leg steak
or neck fillet, cubed
200g/7oz basmati rice, rinsed in
cold water
400ml/14fl oz lamb or chicken stock
200g/7oz fresh spinach

Takes 25 minutes • Serves 4

1 Heat a large pan, add the curry paste and sizzle for a minute until fragrant, then add the lamb and brown it on all sides. Pour in the rice and stock, and stir well. Bring to the boil, cover with a lid, then cook for 15 minutes on a medium heat or until the rice is tender.
2 Stir through the spinach, put the lid back on the pan and leave to steam, undisturbed, for 5 minutes more. Give everything a good stir and bring the dish to the table to let everyone help themselves.

• Per serving 387 kcalories, protein 32g, carbohydrate 41g, fat 12g, saturated fat 5g, fibre 1g, sugar 1g, salt 1.05g

This salad is also great for lunch the next day – if there's any left!

Wild rice and feta salad

250g/9oz basmati and wild rice
400g can chickpeas, drained and rinsed
100g/4oz dried cranberries
1 red onion, sliced
1 garlic clove, crushed
3 tbsp olive oil
2 tbsp fresh lemon juice
200g pack reduced-fat feta
handful of flat-leaf parsley, roughly chopped

Takes 30 minutes • Serves 4

1 Rinse the rice in cold water until the water runs clear. Cook the rice in a pan of boiling water according to the packet instructions, adding the chickpeas for the final 4 minutes. Drain and allow to cool a little, then mix through the cranberries and onion.
2 To make the dressing, whisk together the garlic, olive oil and lemon juice and add some seasoning. Toss with the rice mixture, then pile on to a large serving plate. Crumble over the feta, then scatter with parsley. Serve warm or cold.

• Per serving 519 kcalories, protein 20g, carbohydrate 79g, fat 16g, saturated fat 5g, fibre 4g, sugar 19g, salt 1.82g

A quick and easy recipe to get you through the week – with the added bonus that it's low in fat!

Crab and noodle soup

50g/2oz thin rice noodles
100g/4oz Chinese-style stir-fry mixed vegetables
2 tsp fish sauce
2 tsp sweet chilli sauce
600ml/1 pint vegetable stock
170g can white crabmeat in brine
handful of coriander leaves, roughly chopped

Takes 10 minutes • Serves 2

1 Fill a kettle and bring to the boil. Put the noodles and vegetables into a large bowl, then pour over the boiling water. Leave to soak for 4 minutes or until the noodles are tender and the vegetables just softened.
2 Meanwhile, in a pan, heat together the fish sauce, chilli sauce and stock until simmering, and give them a good stir. Drain the noodles and vegetables of their soaking water, divide between two serving bowls, then crumble over the crabmeat. Pour over the hot stock, scatter with coriander and serve.

• Per serving 184 kcalories, protein 17g, carbohydrate 28g, fat 1g, saturated fat none, fibre 3g, sugar 5g, salt 2.66g

A speedy way to spice up your weekday menu.

Chilli beef noodles

1.5 litres/2¾ pints vegetable stock
6 thin slices fresh root ginger, peeled
1 large red chilli, halved lengthways
1 bunch spring onions, finely sliced
1 sirloin steak, trimmed
1 tbsp sunflower oil
250g pack pak choi, quartered
300g/10oz thin egg noodles

Takes 25 minutes • Serves 2

1 Place the stock, ginger, chilli and spring onions in a large pan and bring to the boil.
2 Meanwhile, heat a griddle pan until very hot and brush the steak with the oil. Griddle the steak for 2 minutes each side for medium–rare/ 4 minutes for well-done. Transfer to a chopping board and leave to rest for 1 minute, then thinly slice.
3 Add the pak choi to the stock, then the noodles, bring to the boil and simmer for 3 minutes or until tender. Ladle the stock, noodles and pak choi into large serving bowls and top with thin slices of steak.

• Per serving 815 kcalories, protein 46g, carbohydrate 114g, fat 23g, saturated fat 3g, fibre 5g, sugar 5g, salt 3.98g

This stress-free exotic meal is conveniently made in just one pan – which also saves time on the washing up!

One-pan prawn pilau

2 tbsp korma curry paste
1 small onion, finely chopped
300g/10oz basmati rice, rinsed and drained
700ml/1¼ pint chicken stock, made from a cube
150g pack cooked peeled prawns (defrosted if frozen)
cupful of frozen peas
1 red chilli, sliced into rings
handful of coriander leaves, chopped, to garnish

Takes 30 minutes, plus defrosting time
Serves 4

1 Heat a large, wide pan and dry–fry the curry paste with the onions for 4–5 minutes or until the onion begins to soften. Add the rice to the pan and stir to coat in the curry paste. Add the stock, then bring to the boil.
2 Cover the pan and turn the heat down to low. Leave the rice to simmer slowly for 12–15 minutes or until all the liquid has been absorbed and the rice is cooked. Turn off the heat and stir in the prawns, peas and chilli. Cover the pan and leave to stand for 5 minutes.
3 Fluff up the rice grains with a fork and season, if you like. Scatter over the coriander and serve with lemon wedges.

• Per serving 340 kcalories, protein 18g, carbohydrate 65g, fat 3g, saturated fat 1g, fibre 2g, added sugar none, salt 2.38g

The perfect supper for those nights when all that's left in the fridge are the basics.

Raid-the-fridge rice

6 rashers rindless streaky or back bacon, chopped
handful of closed-cup mushrooms, halved
1 tbsp sunflower or vegetable oil
1 small onion, chopped
1 garlic clove, crushed
140g/5oz long grain rice
300ml/½ pint hot chicken or vegetable stock, made with a cube
handful of grated Cheddar or other hard cheese

Takes 25 minutes • Serves 2

1 Heat a large, non-stick pan and tip in the bacon. Fry for a few minutes over a medium heat. Add the mushrooms, turn up the heat, then fry for another 3–4 minutes. Tip out on to a plate.
2 In the same pan, heat the oil, then fry the onion for 5 minutes. Add the garlic and fry for another minute, then tip in the rice. Pour in the stock, stir once and bring to the boil. Turn down to a gentle simmer and cook for 10 minutes or until almost all of the liquid has gone. Take off the heat, give it a stir and cover with a lid (or a big plate). Leave for 5 minutes to finish cooking in its own steam.
3 Stir most of the cheese through the rice, then season to taste. Serve in bowls topped with the bacon and mushrooms and the rest of the cheese sprinkled over.

• Per serving 549 kcalories, protein 19g, carbohydrate 68g, fat 24g, saturated fat 9g, fibre 1g, sugar 2g, salt 2.32g

If you haven't tried the healthy grain quinoa before, this is the perfect recipe with which to start.

Spicy vegetable and quinoa laksa

1 onion, sliced
4 tbsp korma or madras curry paste
1 litre/1¾ pints milk
750g/1lb 10oz frozen mixed vegetables
175g/6oz quinoa, rinsed

Takes 20 minutes • Serves 4

1 In a large pan over a medium heat, simmer the onion and the curry paste with a splash of water for 5 minutes, stirring from time to time until the onion has softened. Heat the milk in a jug in the microwave.

2 Add the vegetables and quinoa to the pan, then stir in the milk. Bring everything to the boil, simmer gently for 10 minutes or until the quinoa is cooked, and season with salt and pepper. Serve with warm naan bread.

• Per serving 398 kcalories, protein 22g, carbohydrate 55g, fat 12g, saturated fat 3g, fibre 7g, sugar 4g, salt 0.96g

Adding a little sugar to a tomato-based sauce brings out the natural sweetness of the tomatoes.

Herby bean sausage stew

8 chipolatas
2 × 420g cans mixed beans
2 × 400g cans chopped tomatoes
1 tsp dried basil
2 tsp dried oregano
1 tbsp sugar

Takes 20 minutes • Serves 4

1 Heat a large non-stick frying pan, then brown the sausages on all sides for 3–5 minutes over a high heat.
2 Strain the beans through a sieve and rinse under cold water, then add to the pan with the chopped tomatoes and sprinkle over the herbs and sugar. Season well and bring to the boil. Simmer for 10 minutes, stirring occasionally until the sausages are cooked through and the sauce has thickened and coats the beans. Serve scooped straight from the pan.

• Per serving 355 kcalories, protein 20g, carbohydrate 37g, fat 15g, saturated fat 5g, fibre 10g, sugar 13g, salt 2.68g

This pesto crumb mixture also makes a fantastic topping for chicken breasts or lamb chops.

Pesto and olive-crusted fish

2 tbsp green pesto
finely grated zest of 1 lemon
10 green olives, pitted and roughly chopped
85g/3oz fresh breadcrumbs
4 white fish fillets, such as cod or haddock

Takes 20 minutes • Serves 4

1 Preheat the oven to 200°C/fan 180°C/gas 6. Mix the pesto, lemon zest and olives together, then stir in the breadcrumbs.
2 Lay the fish fillets on a baking sheet, skin side down, then press the crumbs over the surface of each piece. Bake in the oven for 10–12 minutes or until the fish is cooked through and the crust is crisp and brown.

• Per serving 219 kcalories, protein 30g, carbohydrate 17g, fat 4g, saturated fat 1g, fibre 1g, sugar 1g, salt 1.14g

Comfort food in a flash: a fast and tasty shepherd's pie that the whole family will love.

Quick spiced shepherd's pie

4 tbsp olive oil
500g pack minced lamb
3 tbsp garam Masala mix
400g can chopped tomatoes with garlic and onion
750g/1lb 10oz cooked potatoes

Takes 45 minutes • Serves 4

1 Heat one tablespoon of the olive oil in a large non-stick frying pan, then fry the lamb and half the garam Masala over a high heat for 8 minutes until browned. Tip in the tomatoes, then season and simmer for 20 minutes or until thick. Meanwhile, crush the potatoes with the remaining oil and garam Masala.

2 Heat the grill to High. Tip the hot lamb sauce into a gratin dish and scatter with the potatoes. The pie can now be cooled and then frozen for up to a month. Otherwise, grill for 8 minutes or until the potatoes are crispy and golden.

• Per serving 562 kcalories, protein 29g, carbohydrate 41g, fat 33g, saturated fat 11g, fibre 3g, sugar 2g, salt 3.62g

These filo-topped fish fillets are super easy but smart enough for entertaining.

Fish pie fillets

4 × 175g/6oz thick white fish fillets (such as haddock)
1 small bunch dill, leaves only, chopped
100g/4oz half-fat soft cheese
200g/7oz frozen prawns, raw or cooked, defrosted
4 sheets filo pastry
2 tsp sunflower oil
1 tbsp Parmesan, finely grated

Takes 20 minutes, plus defrosting
Makes 4

1 Preheat the oven to 220°C/fan 200°C/gas 7. Put the fish on to a non-stick baking sheet and season all over. Mix the dill and soft cheese in a small bowl, then stir in the prawns, taking care not to break them up. Season with black pepper, then spread evenly over the fish.

2 Brush the filo sheets with the oil, then cut into thick strips. Scrunch the pastry up a little and crumple on top of the fish. Scatter with Parmesan, then bake for 10 minutes or until the fish is cooked through and the pastry is crisp and golden. (If you've used raw prawns, check they're cooked through properly.) Serve with green beans or a salad with your choice of potatoes.

• Per fillet 296 kcalories, protein 46g, carbohydrate 13g, fat 7g, saturated fat 3g, fibre none, sugar 2g, salt 1.3g

For an even quicker version of this recipe, use roasted vegetables bought from the deli counter.

Frying-pan pizza

1 yellow pepper, seeded and cut into chunks
1 courgette, thickly sliced
1 red onion, cut into wedges
225g/8oz self-raising flour
2 tbsp olive oil, plus 1 tsp extra
5 tbsp fresh tomato sauce
50g/2oz strong Cheddar, grated

Takes 45 minutes • Serves 4

1 Preheat the oven to 220°C/fan 200°C/gas 7. Place the pepper, courgette and red onion on a baking sheet and drizzle with one teaspoon of olive oil. Roast in the oven for 20 minutes until beginning to brown. Set aside.
2 Heat the grill to Medium. Season the flour well and mix with the remaining oil and four–five tablespoons of water, enough to form a soft dough. Knead briefly, then roll out on a floured surface to a rough 20cm/8in circle.
3 Transfer the dough to an ovenproof, non-stick frying pan and fry over a medium heat for 5 minutes or until the underside begins to brown. Turn over and fry for 5 minutes.
4 Spread the tomato sauce over the base, scatter with the veg, then sprinkle with cheese. Grill the pizza for 3–4 minutes until the cheese has melted. Slice into wedges.

• Per serving 331 kcalories, protein 10g, carbohydrate 49g, fat 12g, saturated fat 4g, fibre 3g, sugar 6g, salt 0.89g

Here we've taken a slow-cooked classic and made it extra fast.

Quick chicken chasseur

8 rashers rindless streaky bacon,
chopped into large pieces
4 chicken breasts, cut into
large chunks
200g pack baby button mushrooms
1 tbsp plain flour
400g can chopped tomatoes
with garlic
1 beef stock cube
dash of Worcestershire sauce
handful of parsley leaves, chopped

Takes 20 minutes • Serves 4

1 Heat a shallow pan and sizzle the bacon for about 2 minutes until starting to brown. Throw in the chicken, then fry for 3–4 minutes until it has changed colour. Turn up the heat and throw in the mushrooms. Cook for a few minutes, stir in the flour, then cook until a paste forms.

2 Tip in the tomatoes, stir, then crumble in the stock cube. Bubble everything together for 10 minutes, splash in the Worcestershire sauce, stir through the parsley, then serve with mashed potatoes or boiled rice.

• Per serving 298 kcalories, protein 43g, carbohydrate 6g, fat 12g, saturated fat 4g, fibre 2g, sugar 2g, salt 2.65g

An easy-to-prepare, comforting vegetarian main course.

Flageolet bean pie

1 tbsp olive oil
1 onion, finely chopped
3 garlic cloves, crushed
3 × 400g cans flageolet beans,
drained and rinsed
5 tbsp crème fraîche
2 tbsp fresh or 2 tsp dried
thyme leaves
100g/4oz breadcrumbs
50g/2oz vegetarian Cheddar,
grated

Takes 20 minutes • Serves 4

1 Heat the grill to High. Heat the oil in a frying pan and gently fry the onion for about 5 minutes or until softened. Stir in the garlic and cook for another minute. Add the beans, crème fraîche and half the thyme. Season well, then cook until heated through.
2 Mix the breadcrumbs and cheese together, then stir in the rest of the thyme. Pour the bean mix into a baking dish and scatter with the breadcrumbs. Grill until the topping is crisp and golden. Serve scooped straight from the dish with a green salad on the side.

• Per serving 421 kcalories, protein 21g, carbohydrate 49g, fat 17g, saturated fat 8g, fibre 9g, sugar 3g, salt 1.73g

These aromatic chops make a perfect treat for two.

Indian lamb cutlets

50g/2oz Parmesan, finely grated
1 tbsp curry powder
4 lamb cutlets
1 tbsp olive oil

Takes 15 minutes • Serves 2

1 Preheat the oven to 200°C/fan 180°C/ gas 6. Mix the Parmesan and curry powder together. Season the lamb generously with pepper and a little salt, then press the meat into the cheese mix to coat. Heat the oil in an ovenproof frying pan, or heavy baking sheet, and fry the cutlets for 2 minutes on each side to brown.
2 Transfer the cutlets to the oven – 5 minutes for medium-rare. These are delicious served with a dollop of tomato chutney and some mash flavoured with chopped coriander.

• Per serving 611 kcalories, protein 39g, carbohydrate 2g, fat 50g, saturated fat 24g, fibre 2g, sugar none, salt 0.81g

These fun lamb pittas are great hand-held food, perfect for a casual supper.

Turkish-style lamb

4 lamb leg steaks
2 tsp lamb seasoning
1 tsp dried oregano, or mixed herbs
1 small bunch mint, leaves only, chopped
2 × 150g cartons low-fat natural yogurt
4 pitta breads (white or wholemeal)
iceberg lettuce, shredded
1 red onion, thinly sliced
1 lemon, cut into wedges for squeezing (optional)

Takes 20 minutes • Serves 4

1 Heat the grill to High. Season the lamb with salt and pepper, then grill for 2 minutes on each side until browned, but still very rare.
2 Meanwhile, mix the seasoning, oregano (or mixed herbs) and half of the mint into one of the tubs of yogurt, smother this on the lamb, then return to the grill for another 2–3 minutes or until the yogurt is blistered and the meat is cooked to your liking.
3 Leave the meat to rest on a board for a few minutes while you toast the pittas, shred the lettuce and thinly slice the red onion.
4 Stir the rest of the mint into the second tub of yogurt. Thickly slice the meat and stuff pieces into the pitta bread along with some salad and minted yogurt. Add a squeeze of lemon juice before tucking in, if you like.

• Per serving 502 kcalories, protein 48g, carbohydrate 51g, fat 13g, saturated fat 6g, fibre 3g, sugar 9g, salt 1.53g

This speedy low-fat curry involves minimum shopping but delivers maximum flavour. It can be easily doubled for family or friends.

Prawn curry in a hurry

2 tbsp curry paste
1 onion, finely sliced
200g/7oz large raw or cooked prawns, peeled and defrosted if frozen
400g can chopped tomatoes with garlic
1 large bunch coriander, leaves and stalks chopped
boiled rice and naan bread, to serve

Takes 15 minutes, plus any defrosting
Serves 2

1 Drizzle some oil from the curry paste jar into a wok or large frying pan, gently heat, then add the onion. Sizzle over a low heat for 4 minutes or until the onion softens, then stir in the paste and cook for a few minutes longer.

2 Stir in the prawns and tomatoes, then bring to a simmer. If using raw prawns, simmer until they have changed colour and are cooked through. Season to taste. Add the coriander just before serving with boiled rice and naan bread.

• Per serving 166 kcalories, protein 22g, carbohydrate 11g, fat 4g, saturated fat 1g, fibre 3g, sugar 8g, salt 1.08g

When working with filo pastry, cover it with some damp sheets of kitchen paper to stop it drying out as you go along.

Crispy Greek-style pie

200g bag spinach leaves
175g jar sun-dried tomatoes in oil
100g/4oz feta, crumbled
2 eggs, beaten
250g pack filo pastry

Takes 40 minutes • Serves 4

1 Put the spinach into a pan with two tablespoons of water. Cook until wilted. Tip into a sieve, squeeze out any excess water and chop. Chop the tomatoes (reserving the oil) and mix with the spinach, feta and eggs.
2 Preheat the oven to 180°C/fan 160°C/gas 4. Carefully unroll the filo pastry. Take a sheet of pastry and brush liberally with some sun-dried tomato oil. Drape oil-side down in a 22cm/9in loose-bottomed cake tin so that some of the pastry hangs over the side. Brush oil over another piece of pastry and place it in the tin, a little further round. Keep placing the filo sheets in the tin until you have three layers. Spoon over the filling. Pull the sides into the middle, scrunch up completely covering the filling. Brush with a little more oil.
3 Cook the pie for 30 minutes or until the pastry is crisp and golden brown. Remove from the tin, slice into wedges and serve.

• Per serving 260 kcalories, protein 13g, carbohydrate 23g, fat 14g, saturated fat 5g, fibre 3g, sugar 5g, salt 3g

The glaze in this recipe can also be used as a quick stir-fry sauce.

Sweet-glazed pork

2 tsp Chinese 5-spice powder
3 tbsp clear honey
splash of fresh orange juice
4 pork loin steaks or chops, trimmed of fat
4 heads bok choi, halved lengthways

Takes 15 minutes, plus marinating
Serves 4

1 In a small bowl, mix together the 5-spice powder, honey and enough orange juice to loosen, then smear the paste over the chops. Leave to marinate for 10 minutes.
2 Heat the grill to Medium, then grill the chops for 4–5 minutes on each side, basting with any leftover glaze, until cooked through.
3 Steam the bok choi for 2 minutes or until wilted. Serve with the pork chops, drizzled with any juices and glaze from the grill pan.

• Per serving 218 kcalories, protein 32g, carbohydrate 10g, fat 6g, saturated fat 2g, fibre 1g, sugar 10g, salt 0.34g

These fish fillets freeze really well raw with their topping, as long as the fish hasn't been previously frozen.

Curry-crusted fish

3 slices bread (about 85g/3oz in total)
1 tbsp korma curry paste
4 thick white fish fillets
1 lime

Takes 15 minutes • Serves 4

1 Preheat the oven to 200°C/fan 180°C/gas 6. Put the bread into a food processor and whiz until you have rough crumbs. Add the curry paste and whiz again until the crumbs are fairly fine and evenly coated in the curry paste.

2 Put the fish fillets on to a baking sheet, season on both sides, then grate the zest of half the lime on top. Gently press the curry-paste crumbs on top of the fish, then bake until the fish is cooked through and the topping crisp and golden, about 7 minutes. Serve with rice and the lime cut into wedges for squeezing over.

• Per serving 178 kcalories, protein 29g, carbohydrate 11g, fat 2g, saturated fat none, fibre none, sugar 1g, salt 0.64g.

This sauce can be used on burgers and with beef and chicken too.

Lamb steaks with barbecue sauce

4 lamb leg steaks
1 tbsp sunflower oil, plus a little extra
for brushing steaks
1 onion, chopped
150ml/¼pint tomato ketchup
3 tbsp Worcestershire sauce
2 tbsp light muscovado sugar
2 tbsp red wine vinegar

Takes 25 minutes • Serves 4

1 Season the steaks on both sides and brush with a little oil.
2 To make the sauce, heat the remaining oil in a small pan, then add the onion and fry for 10 minutes until soft and lightly browned. Add the remaining ingredients, simmer gently, and stir for 5 minutes more until everything has combined into one sauce.
3 Barbecue, griddle or grill the steaks for 3–4 minutes on each side, or until cooked to your liking, and serve with the sauce on the side.

• Per serving 358 kcalories, protein 38g, carbohydrate 23g, fat 14g, saturated fat 6g, fibre 1g, sugar 21g, salt 2.13g

Smashed pulses make a tasty, nutritious alternative to mashed potato.

Pork with garlicky bean mash

1 pork steak, trimmed of fat
1 tbsp olive oil
1 small onion or shallot, chopped
1 garlic clove, crushed
410g can haricot beans in water, drained and rinsed
125ml/4fl oz vegetable stock
1 tbsp chopped fresh coriander

Takes 20 minutes • Serves 1

1 Heat the grill to High. Lay the pork on a baking sheet and grill the steaks for 12–15 minutes, turning once, until browned and cooked through.
2 Meanwhile, heat the oil in a small pan, add the onion or shallot and fry for 5 minutes until softened. Add the garlic to the pan, fry for 1 minute more, then tip in the beans and stock and simmer for 5 minutes more. Roughly mash the beans with a potato masher or fork, then stir in the coriander. Serve the pork with the hot bean mash on the side.

• Per serving 444 kcalories, protein 42g, carbohydrate 30g, fat 18g, saturated fat 3g, fibre 9g, sugar 7g, salt 0.39g

This delicious marinade also works really well on barbecued chicken wings.

Sticky chicken drumsticks

8 chicken drumsticks
2 tbsp soy sauce
1 tbsp honey
1 tbsp olive oil
1 tsp tomato purée
1 tbsp Dijon mustard

Takes 40 minutes • Serves 4

1 Make three slashes on each of the drumsticks. Mix together the soy sauce, honey, oil, tomato purée and mustard. Pour this mixture over the chicken and coat thoroughly. Leave to marinate for 30 minutes at room temperature or overnight in the fridge.

2 Preheat the oven to 200°C/fan 180°C/gas 6. Tip the chicken into a shallow roasting tin and cook for 35 minutes, turning occasionally, or until the chicken is tender and glistening with the marinade.

• Per serving 267 kcalories, protein 32g, carbohydrate 4g, fat 14g, saturated fat 4g, fibre none, sugar 4g, salt 2.04g

The lime pickle used in this recipe is quite spicy, so add it a little at a time, tasting the sauce as you go along.

Spicy coconut and pumpkin curry

1 piece pumpkin (about
1kg/2lb 4oz)
100ml/3½fl oz coconut cream
1–2 tbsp red curry paste
25g/1oz light brown sugar
400ml can coconut milk
10 kaffir lime leaves
1 tbsp fish sauce
50g/2oz hot green mango chutney
100g/4oz hot lime pickle
100g/4oz beansprouts
small handful of mint leaves, to serve

Takes 40 minutes • Serves 4

1 Peel the pumpkin, scoop out the seeds with a teaspoon and cut into thick wedges. Heat a wok. Add half the coconut cream and cook over a high heat until it splits and the oil separates.
2 Add the red curry paste and fry for about 2 minutes until fragrant. Add the sugar and cook for 3 minutes more, then stir in the pumpkin and cook for 4–5 minutes so that it's well coated in the spices. Add the coconut milk and the remaining coconut cream and bring to the boil. Add the lime leaves, then turn down the heat and leave to simmer for 20 minutes. Stir in the fish sauce to taste then add the chutney and the lime pickle.
3 Serve topped with the bean sprouts, mint, and some plain rice.

• Per serving 438 kcalories, protein 7g, carbohydrate 38g, fat 30g, saturated fat 22g, fibre 4g, sugar 28g, salt 1.94g

Give the Sunday roast an Asian twist with this crispy-skinned Peking chicken recipe.

Peking-style chicken

1 orange
5 tbsp soy sauce
3 tbsp dry sherry
1 tsp Chinese 5-spice powder
4 garlic cloves
thumb-sized piece fresh root ginger
1 whole chicken
2 tbsp honey

Takes 1½ hour, plus marinating
Serves 6

1 Pare the zest from the orange in thick strips then mix with the soy sauce, sherry and 5-spice powder. Bash the garlic and ginger, add to the sauce and mix well. Rub all over the chicken (retaining the ginger and garlic) and marinate in the fridge for 3 hours.
2 Preheat the oven to 190°C/fan 170°C/gas 5. Remove the chicken from the marinade. Halve the orange and put inside the cavity along with the ginger and garlic from the marinade. Set the chicken on a wire rack over a roasting tin. Roast for 50 minutes per kg until the juices run clear when pierced with a skewer at the thickest point.
3 Strain the marinade into a pan along with the honey. Bring to the boil then simmer for a 2 minutes. Just before serving, turn the oven up as high as it will go. Brush marinade all over the chicken, return it to the oven and cook until the chicken is crisp and browned.

• Per serving 235 kcalories, protein 21g, carbohydrate 5g, fat 14g, saturated fat 5g, fibre none, sugar 5g, salt 2.26g

Although this recipe feels summery, it can be enjoyed any time of year.

Houmous-crusted lamb with lentil salad

8 lamb cutlets or small chops
200g tub houmous

FOR THE SALAD
410g can puy lentils, drained and
rinsed
175g/6oz roasted peppers from a jar,
drained and sliced
100g bag baby leaf spinach
2 tbsp olive oil
2 tbsp lemon juice
2 tsp Dijon mustard

Takes 20 minutes • Serves 4

1 Make the salad: in a bowl, combine the lentils, roasted peppers and spinach. In a separate small bowl, whisk together the oil, lemon juice and mustard to make a dressing, then stir into the lentils.

2 Heat the grill to High and season the lamb generously with pepper and sparingly with a little salt. Grill for 3 minutes on each side, then spoon one heaped teaspoon of houmous on top of each cutlet. Grill for another minute or until the houmous starts to turn golden.

3 Serve with the lentil salad, any extra houmous and some toasted pitta bread.

• Per serving 541 kcalories, protein 31g, carbohydrate 14g, fat 41g, saturated fat 17g, fibre 4g, sugar 3g, salt 2.03g

Dried porcini mushrooms make this treat for two a must-try for steak lovers.

Porcini-rubbed steak

25g/1oz dried porcini mushrooms
1 sprig fresh thyme, leaves only
2 thick sirloin steaks
1 tbsp olive oil
baked potatoes and green salad, to serve

Takes 10 minutes • Serves 2

1 Whiz the mushrooms into a fine powder in a small food processor or coffee grinder. Mix with a good pinch of salt, pepper and the thyme leaves. Rub the mixture all over the steaks, then pop them on to a plate or into a sealable kitchen bag and chill overnight.
2 Brush away any excess mixture from the steaks. Heat a griddle pan until smoking hot, turn the heat to Medium, then smear a little olive oil over one side of each steak. Griddle, oiled-side down, for 3 minutes. Turn over (there's no need to oil the other side), then cook for another 2 minutes for medium–rare, 4 minutes for well-done. Serve with a baked potato and salad.

• Per serving 428 kcalories, protein 47g, carbohydrate 1g, fat 26g, saturated fat 10g, fibre 2g, sugar none, salt 0.29g

A low-fat, quick casserole that's as easy to make for a crowd, or for the freezer, as it is for one.

Squash and chorizo stew

140g/5oz chorizo sausage, thickly sliced
1 onion, chopped
680g jar passata
1 butternut squash (approx. 1kg/2lb 4oz), peeled and cut into 1–2cm chunks
handful of flat-leaf parsley, chopped

Takes 35 minutes • Serves 4

1 Heat a large pan, add the chorizo, then cook over a high heat for 2 minutes or until it starts to release its red oil. Lift the chorizo out of the pan, then add the onion and fry for 5 minutes until starting to soften.
2 Tip in the passata, squash and chorizo, bring to the boil, then cover and cook for 15–20 minutes or until the squash is softened, but not broken up. If you need to, add a little water during cooking. Season to taste, then serve in bowls scattered with parsley.

• Per serving 264 kcalories, protein 13g, carbohydrate 35g, fat 9g, saturated fat 4g, fibre 5g, sugar 19g, salt 2.17g

Everybody loves fishcakes, and these mouth-watering morsels are a healthy version, containing the super-food beetroot.

Crisp fishcakes with beetroot

500g/1lb 2oz cooked potatoes
4 spring onions, finely chopped
200g/7oz cooked beetroot, finely chopped
170g can salmon in brine, drained
1 tbsp sunflower oil

Takes 20 minutes • Serves 4

1 Put the potatoes into a bowl and mash roughly with a fork. Add the onions, beetroot, salt and pepper, then mash everything together. Flake the salmon, then stir into the mix. Using your hands, shape the mixture into eight rough patties.

2 Heat the oil in a large non-stick frying pan and add the fishcakes. Fry on a fairly high heat until the underside is brown and crusty. Flip over and cook on the other side. (If you need to do this in two batches, keep the first batch warm while cooking the second.) Serve with salad.

• Per serving 197 kcalories, protein 11g, carbohydrate 26g, fat 6g, saturated fat 1g, fibre 3g, sugar 6g, salt 0.72g

A spicy, filling one-pot that's quicker to cook than a ready-meal.

Lemon-spiced chicken with chickpeas

1 tbsp sunflower oil
1 onion, halved and thinly sliced
4 boneless skinless chicken breasts, cut into chunks
1 cinnamon stick, broken in half
1 tsp each ground coriander and cumin
zest and juice of 1 lemon
400g can chickpeas, drained and rinsed
200ml/7fl oz chicken stock
250g bag spinach

Takes 20 minutes • Serves 4

1 Heat the oil in a large frying pan, then fry the onion gently for 5 minutes. Turn up the heat and add the chicken, frying for about 3 minutes or until golden. Stir in the spices and lemon zest, fry for 1 more minute, then tip in the chickpeas and stock. Put the lid on and simmer for everything for 5 minutes.
2 Season to taste, then tip in the spinach and re-cover. Leave the spinach to wilt for 2 minutes, then stir it through the chicken. Squeeze over the lemon juice just before serving.

• Per serving 290 kcalories, protein 42g, carbohydrate 14g, fat 7g, saturated fat 1g, fibre 4g, sugar 3g, salt 1.03g

Wasabi paste is a hot condiment that's a little like horseradish. If you can't get hold of any, use English mustard or horseradish sauce instead.

Soy tuna with wasabi mash

3 tbsp soy sauce
1 tbsp rice wine vinegar
1 tbsp caster sugar
2 tuna steaks (about 140g/5oz)
500g/1lb 2oz potatoes
100ml/3½fl oz semi-skimmed milk
2 tsp wasabi paste
1 spring onion, finely sliced
frozen broad beans or soya beans, to serve

Takes 25 minutes • Serves 2

1 Mix together the soy sauce, vinegar and sugar. Pour over the tuna and marinate for at least 20 minutes or up to 2 hours in the fridge.
2 Place the potatoes in a pan of lightly salted boiling water, then cook for 10–15 minutes or until soft. Drain well. Heat the milk in the pan and mix in the wasabi. Return the potatoes to the pan, then mash until smooth. Stir through the spring onion and keep warm.
3 Heat a non-stick griddle pan until smoking hot. Remove the tuna from the marinade and cook on the griddle for 2–3 minutes each side, or until seared on the outside but still pink inside.
4 Cook the broad or soya beans according to the packet instructions, then serve alongside the tuna and mash.

• Per serving 439 kcalories, protein 43g, carbohydrate 51g, fat 9g, saturated fat 2g, fibre 3g, sugar 7g, salt 1.38g

Pronounced ba-boor-tea, the national dish of South Africa is a mixture of curried meat and fruit topped with an egg custard – not dissimilar to the Greek moussaka.

Bobotie

2 slices white bread
2 onions, chopped
25g/1oz butter
2 garlic cloves, crushed
1 kg packet lean minced beef
2 tbsp madras curry paste
1 tsp dried mixed herbs
3 cloves
5 allspice berries
2 tbsp peach mango chutney
3 tbsp sultanas
6 bay leaves

FOR THE TOPPING
300ml/½ pint full fat milk
2 large eggs

Takes 1 hour 10 minutes • Serves 6

1 Preheat the oven to 180°C/fan 160°C/ gas 4. Pour cold water over the bread and set aside to soak.
2 Fry the onions in butter for 10 minutes or until they are soft. Add the garlic and beef. Stir well, crushing the mince into fine grains as it browns. Stir in the curry paste, herbs, spices, chutney, sultanas and 2 bay leaves, a teaspoon of salt and plenty of black pepper.
3 Cover and simmer for 10 minutes. Squeeze the water from the bread, then beat the bread into the meat mixture. Tip into an ovenproof dish. Press the mixture down well.
4 For the topping, beat the milk and eggs with seasoning, then pour over the meat. Top with the remaining bay leaves and bake for 35–40 minutes or until the topping is set and starting to turn golden. Serve with a salad.

• Per serving 386 kcalories, protein 43g, carbohydrate 20g, fat 16g, saturated fat 6g, fibre 1g, sugar 3g, salt 0.97g

A healthy supper that's full of flavour and on the table in less than half an hour.

Fish with spiced lentils

1 lime, cut into quarters
3 tbsp sunflower or vegetable oil
1 onion, chopped
1 tbsp medium curry powder
1 tbsp tomato purée
400g can green or brown lentils, drained, rinsed, and drained again
2 tbsp mango chutney, plus extra to serve
4 × 140g/5oz white fish fillets
naan bread or chapatis, to serve

Takes 25 minutes • Serves 4

1 Finely chop one of the lime quarters, including the skin. Heat two tablespoons of oil in a medium pan then fry the onion over a medium heat for 5 minutes until softened and starting to colour. Add the curry powder and tomato purée then fry for another minute. Tip in 200ml/7fl oz water, the lentils, mango chutney and the chopped lime, then bring to the boil. Simmer for 5 minutes or until thickened.

2 Heat the remaining oil in a frying pan. Season the fish with salt and pepper to taste then fry for 5 minutes, turning halfway through, until golden and cooked through. Add a squeeze of lime to the pan and to the lentils then serve together with naan bread or chapatis on the side.

• Per serving 273 kcalories, protein 31g, carbohydrate 16g, fat 10g, saturated fat 1g, fibre 3g, sugar 9g, salt 1.33g

A rich and warming one-pot casserole for a solo supper that can be easily doubled.

20-minute beef in red wine

1 tbsp olive oil
200g/7oz sirloin or rump steak
1 small onion, sliced
1 garlic clove, finely sliced
pinch of dried oregano
1 glass red wine
200g can chopped tomatoes

Takes 20 minutes • Serves 1

1 Heat the oil in a pan and fry the steak for 2 minutes on each side or until browned. Remove the steak to a plate, then throw the onion, garlic and oregano into the pan. Fry for 5 minutes until starting to turn golden.
2 Tip the wine and tomatoes into the pan, then simmer for 10 minutes until thickened and rich. Slice the steak into chunks, return to the pan with any juices, then simmer for a few minutes to reheat. Serve with pasta, chips or sauté potatoes.

• Per serving 619 kcalories, protein 47g, carbohydrate 16g, fat 37g, saturated fat 13g, fibre 3g, sugar 13g, salt 0.74g

An intimate supper for two, or you can simply double the recipe if you have friends over. If you haven't got any tarragon, use dill or basil instead.

Pancetta-wrapped salmon

200g/7oz small new potatoes, sliced
3 fresh tarragon sprigs, leaves chopped
zest of 1 lemon
knob of butter
2 × 175g/6oz skinless salmon fillets
4 slices pancetta or prosciutto
green beans, to serve

Takes 35 minutes • Serves 2

1 Preheat the oven to 200°C/fan 180°C/gas 6.
2 Boil the potatoes for 5 minutes, then drain and tip into a bowl – they will be slightly underdone. Toss with the tarragon, lemon zest, butter and seasoning to taste. Pile in the centre of a foil-lined baking sheet.
3 Season the salmon with black pepper and wrap the pancetta or prosciutto around the fillets. Place them on top of the potatoes and roast for 15–20 minutes, or until the fish flakes easily and the pancetta or prosciutto is golden. Serve with steamed green beans and new potatoes.

• Per serving 455 kcalories, protein 41g, carbohydrate 16g, fat 25g, saturated fat 7g, fibre 1g, sugar 1g, salt 0.93g

Take five ingredients and whip up this quick, healthy vegetarian curry.

Chunky vegetable curry

2 tbsp madras curry paste
1 large butternut squash (600g/1lb 5oz peeled weight), chopped into medium-sized chunks
1 red pepper, halved, seeded and roughly chopped into chunks
400g can reduced-fat coconut milk
1 small bunch fresh coriander, leaves roughly chopped, to garnish
naan bread, to serve

Takes 30 minutes • Serves 2

1 Heat a large frying pan or wok, tip in the curry paste and fry for 1 minute until fragrant. Add the squash and red pepper, then toss well in the paste.
2 Pour over the coconut milk with 200ml/ 7fl oz water and bring everything to a simmer. Cook for 15–20 minutes or until the butternut squash is very tender and the sauce has thickened. Season to taste, then serve the curry scattered with the chopped coriander and naan bread or rice.

• Per serving 458 kcalories, protein 7g, carbohydrate 35g, fat 33g, saturated fat 28g, fibre 6g, sugar 28g, salt 0.64g

This freezable one-pot is the ideal make-ahead meal for a crowd.

Beef and bean hotpot

750g/1lb 10oz lean minced beef
1 beef stock cube
2 large onions, roughly chopped
450g/1lb carrots, peeled and thickly sliced
1.25kg/2lb 12oz potatoes, peeled and cut into large chunks
2 × 400g cans baked beans
Worcestershire sauce or Tabasco sauce, to taste
large handful of parsley, roughly chopped

Takes 1 hour • Serves 8

1 Heat a large non-stick pan, add the beef then fry over a medium-high heat until browned, stirring often and breaking up any lumps with a spoon. Crumble in the stock cube and mix well.
2 Add the vegetables, stir to mix with the beef and pour in enough boiling water (about 1.2 litres/2 pints) to cover. Bring to the boil, then lower the heat and stir well. Cover the pan and simmer gently for about 30 minutes or until the vegetables are tender.
3 Tip in the baked beans, sprinkle with Worcestershire sauce or Tabasco to taste, stir well and heat through. Taste for seasoning and sprinkle with parsley. Serve with extra Worcestershire sauce or Tabasco, if you like a peppery, hot flavour.

• Per serving 362 kcalories, protein 31g, carbohydrate 51g, fat 5g, saturated fat 2g, fibre 8g, sugar 3g, salt 2.05g

This moreish and comforting pudding is a brilliant way to round off a meal.

Nutty apricot and cinnamon puddings

6 Medjool dates, stoned and roughly chopped
handful of chopped dried apricots
1 tsp ground spice
2 tbsp honey
150ml/¼ pint orange fresh juice
handful of chopped mixed nuts
1 Madeira shop-bought cake (loaf)

Takes 20 minutes • Makes 4

1 Put the dates in a small pan with the apricots, spice and honey, then pour over the orange juice. Bring to the boil and cook for 5 minutes or until the dates have broken down and you have a thick, syrupy sauce. Stir in the nuts.

2 Cut the cake in half lengthways, on the horizontal. Use a 150ml/½ pint ramekin to cut out four circles from the cake. Divide the date mix among the four ramekins, then top with the circles of cake, pressing them down gently. Cover with cling film and microwave on High for 3 minutes, then turn out on to a plate and serve with cream or ice cream.

• Per serving 479 kcalories, protein 7g, carbohydrate 83g, fat 15g, saturated fat 7g, fibre 4g, sugar 63g, salt 0.82g

Turn a can of lychees into a non-fat fragrant dessert. A perfect ending to any meal.

Refreshing lychee and lime sorbet

3 x 400g cans lychees in syrup
50g/2oz caster sugar
1 egg white
zest of 2 limes, juice of 1

Takes 15 minutes • Serves 6

1 Drain the syrup from two cans of lychees into a small pan. Add the sugar and dissolve over a gentle heat. Bring to the boil for 1 minute.
2 Blitz the drained lychees in a food processor until very finely chopped. Pour in the lime juice and syrup while the blade is still whirring. (Don't worry if the mix isn't perfectly smooth at this point.) Tip into a 1-litre/¾ pint container and freeze for at least 6 hours until solid.
3 Break up the frozen mixture, then return it to the processor. Tip in the egg white and whiz until thick, pale and smooth. Stir in the zest of one lime. Return to the container and freeze again, ideally overnight. Serve in scoops with the remaining lychees scattered over with the remaining lime zest.

• Per serving 137 kcalories, protein 16g, carbohydrate 35g, fat none, saturated fat none, fibre 1g, sugar 35g, salt 0.04g

This simple idea makes a great midweek pudding.

Honey-nut crunch pears

4 ripe pears
knobs of butter
mixed spice
2 tbsp clear honey
50g/2oz cornflakes
25g/1oz flaked toasted almonds

Takes 15 minutes • Serves 4

1 Preheat the oven to 200°C/fan 180°C/ gas 6. Cut the pears in half lengthways and take out the core, then top with a small knob of butter and a sprinkling of the mixed spice. Sit the pears in a shallow baking dish, then roast for 5 minutes or until starting to soften. Meanwhile, heat the honey and another knob of butter in a large bowl in the microwave for 30 seconds. Toss with the cornflakes and almonds.
2 Take the pears out of the oven, then top with the cornflake mix. Cook for another 5 minutes or until the cornflakes take on a rich golden colour. Allow to cool for a few minutes (the cornflakes crisp up again as they cool), then serve warm with ice cream.

• Per serving 179 kcalories, protein 3g, carbohydrate 31g, fat 6g, saturated fat 1g, fibre 4g, sugar 21g, salt 0.37g

This stunning shortcake takes next to no time to throw together and only has four ingredients.

Fruit custard shortcake

320g pack scone mix
250g pack frozen mixed berries
2 tbsp demerara sugar
500g carton ready-made fresh custard

Takes 15 minutes • Serves 4

1 Preheat the oven to 220°C/fan 200°C/ gas 7. Make up the scone mix according to the packet instructions, then press out into a circle approximately 20cm/8in across on a lightly floured baking sheet. Make the edge a little thicker than the middle. Bake for 10 minutes or until risen and light golden.

2 Meanwhile, put the fruit and sugar in a shallow baking dish and microwave on High for 5 minutes until hot, but the berries are still holding their shape. Heat the custard according to the packet instructions.

3 Spoon a layer of the custard on to the scone base, then top with the drained fruit. Serve with the remaining custard.

• Per serving 475 kcalories, protein 12g, carbohydrate 80g, fat 15g, saturated fat 6g, fibre 3g, sugar 21g, salt 1.19g

This quick low-fat pud is simple to make and can be readily adapted to include your favourite fruit.

Fruity coconut creams

1×50g sachet coconut cream
500g carton 0% Greek yogurt or quark
85g/3oz icing sugar, sieved
2 kiwi fruit
400g can pineapple chunks

Takes 10 minutes • Serves 4

1 Dissolve the coconut cream in 50ml/2fl oz boiling water and leave to cool. Spoon the Quark or yogurt into a mixing bowl, then stir in the icing sugar. Combine with the coconut mix, then spoon into individual glasses. Chill until ready to serve.

2 Peel and chop the kiwi fruit into small pieces. Drain the pineapple chunks and chop them into small pieces. Mix the fruit together, then spoon over the top of the coconut creams to serve.

• Per serving 266 kcalories, protein 19g, carbohydrate 40g, fat 5g, saturated fat 4g, fibre 1g, sugar 39g, salt 0.16g

A quick Easter tart that's delicious at any time of year.

Simnel tart

200g/7oz dried mixed fruits
zest and juice of 1 small orange
1 x 375g sheet ready-rolled
puff pastry
3 tbsp apricot jam
200g/7oz marzipan

Takes 35 minutes • Serves 4

1 Mix the fruit, orange zest and juice in a bowl until completely combined. Unroll the pastry on to a baking sheet. Mark a border 2cm/¾in from the edge with a knife, brush jam over the inside section, then chill for 10 minutes.

2 Preheat the oven to 220°C/fan 200°C/gas 7. Drain the fruit, then stir in the crumbled marzipan. Scatter the fruit mix inside the border. Bake for 20 minutes or until the pastry is golden. Cut into squares and serve with vanilla ice cream or crème fraîche.

• Per serving 713 kcalories, protein 9g, carbohydrate 112g, fat 29g, saturated fat 9g, fibre 2g, sugar 78g, salt 0.84g

The sorbet-like fruit-smoothie mix will make more than you need for four servings, but you can freeze the rest for another day.

Quick iced-fruit meringues

250g bag frozen smoothie mix
200g carton low-fat fromage frais
2 tbsp icing sugar, or to taste
100g punnet blueberries
1 or 2 bananas, sliced
4 small meringue nests

Takes 10 minutes, plus defrosting
Makes 4

1 Tip the smoothie mix into a food processor 10 minutes before you want to use it. Spoon in two tablespoons of the fromage frais and the icing sugar, then whiz until you have a smooth and creamy sorbet-like mix. (If your fruit is still a little too frozen, add one teaspoon of water and whiz again.)
2 Stir in most of the blueberries and the banana, then scoop the mixture on to the meringues. Top with the rest of the fromage frais and decorate with the remaining fruit.

• Per meringue 175 kcalories, protein 5g, carbohydrate 40g, fat none, saturated fat none, fibre 2g, sugar 39g, salt 0.21g.

This no-cook pudding really couldn't be easier or quicker.

Lemon syllabub

284ml carton whipping cream
50g/2oz caster sugar
50ml/2fl oz white wine
zest and juice of 1 lemon
almond thins or fresh berries,
to serve

Takes 10 minutes • Serves 4

1 In a large bowl, whip the cream and sugar together until soft peaks form. Gently stir in the wine, most of the lemon zest and all of the juice until completely combined.
2 Spoon the syllabub into four glasses or bowls, sprinkle with the remaining zest and serve with almond thins or fresh berries.

• Per serving 328 kcalories, protein 2g, carbohydrate 15g, fat 29g, saturated fat 18g, fibre none, sugar 15g, salt 0.05g

Here's a quick, fruity twist on the dessert classic crème brûlée.

Peach and almond crunch

4 ripe peaches
6 amaretti biscuits
2 x 200ml cartons low-fat crème fraîche
85–100g/3–4oz demerara sugar

Takes 15 minutes • Serves 4

1 Heat the grill to High. Stone and slice the peaches. Place the biscuits in a plastic food bag and crush them with a rolling pin.
2 Arrange the peaches and the crumbled biscuits in the bottom of an ovenproof dish. Spoon over the crème fraîche, smooth with a knife so the peaches are entirely covered, then sprinkle over enough sugar to cover the crème fraîche.
3 Place the dish under the grill for 3 minutes or until the sugar has caramelized.

• Per serving 326 kcalories, protein 5g, carbohydrate 44g, fat 16g, saturated fat 10g, fibre 2g, sugar 37g, salt 0.21g

Treat yourself to a delightfully easy family dessert that's ready in minutes.

Lemon curd and yogurt fool

300g jar lemon curd
500g carton 0% Greek yogurt
200g punnet raspberries
1 tbsp icing sugar
shortbread, to serve

Takes 5 minutes • Serves 4

1 Spoon the lemon curd straight from the jar into a bowl and then dollop over the yogurt. Fold the curd and yogurt gently together for a rippled effect. Divide the mixture among four glasses and chill.
2 In another bowl, mix the raspberries and icing sugar together and gently crush them so the fruit starts to release its juices but still has some shape. Spoon the raspberries with their juices over the chilled lemon-yogurt mix, and serve.

• Per serving 299 kcalories, protein 16g, carbohydrate 42g, fat 9g, saturated fat 5g, fibre 1g, sugar 41g, salt 0.66g

Spice up your plums with this simple pudding recipe that cries out for lashings of custard.

Crunchy spiced plums

2 tbsp sugar
2 whole star anise
8 large or 12 small plums, halved
knob of butter
4 HobNob biscuits
custard or vanilla ice cream, to serve

Takes 20 minutes • Serves 4

1 Preheat the oven to 200°C/fan 180°C/gas 6. Mix the sugar with two tablespoons of water in a baking dish, add the star anise, then pop in the plums, cut side down. (They should fit quite snugly.) Dot with the butter and roast for about 5 minutes or until the plums are starting to soften on the bottom, then turn them over. Roast for another 5 minutes or until tender (the time taken will depend on how ripe your fruit is).
2 Roughly crush the HobNobs, then spoon a little on top of each plum half. Return to the oven for a few minutes more until the biscuit topping takes on a dark gold colour. Serve the plums and their scented, syrupy juices with custard or ice cream.

• Per serving 169 kcalories, protein 2g, carbohydrate 31g, fat 5g, saturated fat 2g, fibre 3g, sugar 25g, salt 0.18g

The filling of this tart ends up like a gorgeous, sweet coconut macaroon. Serve with cream or real vanilla ice cream.

Coconut tart

½ tsp ground cinnamon
4 cardamom pods, shelled and seeds crushed
175g/6oz desiccated coconut
225g/8oz caster sugar
¾in × 500g block all-butter shortcrust pastry
plain flour, for dusting
1 egg, beaten
25g/1oz butter, melted
Cape gooseberries (physalis), to serve (optional)

Takes 1 hr 10 minutes • Serves 8

1 Preheat the oven to 200°C/fan 180°C/gas 6. Place a shallow 23cm/9in flan tin on a baking sheet. Tip the spices, coconut and sugar into a pan with 150ml/5fl oz water and cook over a low heat for about 5 minutes, stirring frequently to ensure the mixture doesn't catch. Set aside to cool.
2 Meanwhile, roll out the pastry on a lightly floured surface and use it to line the flan tin. Trim off the excess, fill the pastry case with baking parchment and baking beans and cook for 15 minutes. Remove the beans and cook for 5 minutes more.
3 Beat the egg and melted butter into the cooled coconut mixture, then spoon into the pastry case and smooth the top. Bake for 25 minutes or until the pastry is golden and the coconut a pale gold.

• Per slice 567 kcalories, protein 6g, carbohydrate 62g, fat 35g, saturated fat 20g, fibre 5g, sugar 32g, salt 0.73g

Give your ice cream an Italian twist with this easy dessert.

Hot coffee creams

8 sponge fingers or cantuccini
biscuits
4 tbsp Marsala or dessert wine
500g carton vanilla or coffee
ice cream
150ml/¼ pint strong fresh coffee

Takes 10 minutes, plus soaking time
Serves 4

1 Place two sponge fingers or cantuccini biscuits into the bottom of each of four individual dessert glasses or tumblers. Pour over one tablespoon of the Marsala or dessert wine and leave to soak for a few moments.

2 When ready to serve, remove the ice cream from the freezer and make a fresh pot of hot coffee either in a cafetière, filter machine or percolator. Place a large scoop of ice cream in each glass. Just before eating, pour over a little hot coffee.

• Per serving 273 kcalories, protein 5g, carbohydrate 34g, fat 13g, saturated fat 8g, fibre none, sugar 29g, salt 0.22g

This deceptively simple pudding can be created even faster
by using a microwave.

White chocolate and berry pudding

100g/4oz butter, softened
100g/4oz light brown soft sugar
100g/4oz self-raising flour
2 eggs
3 tbsp milk
85g/3oz white chocolate drops
300g pack frozen mixed berries
icing sugar and custard, to serve

Takes 25 minutes • Serves 4

1 Lightly butter a 1-litre/ 1¾ pint microwavable gratin dish or a 20cm/8in microwave cake dish. Beat together the butter, sugar, flour, eggs and milk with an electric hand whisk for 2–3 minutes or until light and fluffy.

2 Fold through the white chocolate and most of the berries, pour into the dish, then microwave on High for 10–12 minutes or until set and dry on top. Leave to stand for 5 minutes, before dusting with icing sugar and serving with the reserved berries and custard.

3 If you don't have a microwave, bake at 180°C/fan 160°C/gas 4 for 20 minutes or until the cake mixture is risen and golden.

• Per serving 550 kcalories, protein 9g, carbohydrate 63g, fat 31g, saturated fat 18g, fibre 3g, sugar 38g, salt 0.83g

To turn this chilled pudding into a hot dessert, just assemble in microwave-proof bowls and heat for a few minutes before serving.

Apple and blackberry rice

425g can rice pudding
185g jar good-quality apple sauce
150g punnet blackberries (or use frozen and defrost)
2 tbsp light brown soft sugar

Takes 10 minutes, plus defrosting
Serves 4

1 In four small dessert bowls or glasses, layer the rice pudding, apple sauce and blackberries, finishing with a few blackberries on top.

2 Scatter with the brown sugar and chill for 10 minutes or until the sugar has dissolved. You can make these up to 2 hours ahead and keep them, covered, in the fridge.

• Per serving 175 kcalories, protein 4g, carbohydrate 39g, fat 2g, saturated fat 1g, fibre 2g, sugar 31g, salt 0.14g

Index

Picture credits and recipe credits

BBC *Good Food* magazine and BBC Books would like to thank the following people for providing photos. While every effort has been made to trace and acknowledge all photographers, we should like to apologize should there be any errors or omissions.

Peter Cassidy p13, p185; Will Heap p17, p31, p53, p55, p77, p79, p81, p115, p117, p163, p173, p175, p177, p179, p181, p183, p207, p211; Gareth Morgans p6, p11, p15, p19, p21, p23, p25, p27, p29, p35, p37, p43, p51, p57, p59, p61, p63, p65, p67, p69, p71, p83, p85, p87, p89, p91, p93, p95, p97, p99, p101, p105, p121, p123, p125, p127, p129, p131, p133, p135, p137, p139, p141, p143, p145, p147, p149, p155, p187, p189, p191, p193, p195, p197, p199, p201, p203, p205, p209; David Munns p41, p73; Noel Murphy p103; Myles New p39, p45, p47, p75, p107, p109, p111, p113, p151, p153, p159, p165, p167, p169; Lis Parsons p33, p118; Philip Webb p157, p161, p170; Simon Wheeler p49

All the recipes in this book were created by the editorial team at *Good Food* and by regular contributors to the magazine.